Student Companion

enVision® Geometry
Common Core

SAVVAS
LEARNING COMPANY

ISBN-13: 978-1-418-40190-0
ISBN-10:   1-418-40190-0

Contents

enVision Geometry Common Core

About the Authors

Authors

Dan Kennedy, Ph.D

- Retired teacher and Lupton Distinguished Professor of Mathematics at the Baylor School, Chattanooga, TN
- Co-author of textbooks Precalculus: Graphical, Numerical, Algebraic and Calculus: Graphical, Numerical, Algebraic, AP Edition
- Past chair of the College Board's AP Calculus Development Committee
- Previous Tandy Technology Scholar and Presidential Award winner

Eric Milou, Ed.D

- Professor of Mathematics, Rowan University, Glassboro, NJ
- Past President, Association of Mathematics Teachers of New Jersey
- Co-author of *Invigorating High School Math*
- Co-author of NCTM's Catalyzing Change in the Middle School
- Member of the author team for Savvas' **enVision** 6-8
- Past recipient of the Max Sobel Outstanding Mathematics Educator Award

Christine D. Thomas, Ph.D

- Professor of Mathematics Education at Georgia State University, Atlanta, GA
- Past–President of the Association of Mathematics Teacher Educators (AMTE)
- Past NCTM Board of Directors Member
- Past member of the editorial panel of the NCTM journal Mathematics Teacher
- Past co-chair of the steering committee of the North American chapter of the International Group of the Psychology of Mathematics Education

Rose Mary Zbiek, Ph.D

- Professor of Mathematics Education, Pennsylvania State University, College Park, PA
- Series editor for the NCTM *Essential Understanding* project

Contributing Author

Al Cuoco, Ph.D

- Lead author of CME Project, a NSF funded high school curriculum
- Team member to revise the Conference Board of the Mathematical Sciences (CBMS) recommendations for teacher preparation and professional development
- Co-author of several books published by the Mathematical Association of America and the American Mathematical Society
- Consultant to the writers of the Common Core State Standards for Mathematics and the PARCC Content Frameworks for high school
- Recipient of Mary P. Dolciani Award for contributions to the mathematical education of K-16 students

EXPLORE & REASON

A teacher labels two points on the number line.

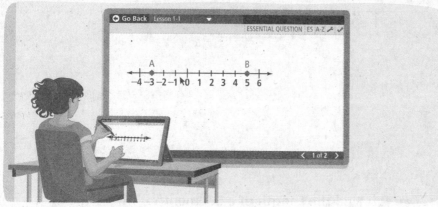

A. What are some methods for finding the distance between points *A* and *B*?

B. Construct Arguments Which method of finding the distance is the best? Explain. © MP.3

HABITS OF MIND

Generalize Which strategy could you apply to find the distance between any two numbers on the number line? © MP.8

EXAMPLE 1

Try It! Find Segment Lengths

1. Refer to the figure. How can you find the length of $\overline{AC}$?

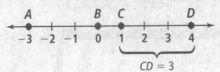

EXAMPLE 2

Try It! Find the Length of a Segment

2. Refer to the figure.

a. What is JK?   b. What is KM?

EXAMPLE 3

Try It! Use the Segment Addition Postulate

3. Points J, K, and L are collinear.

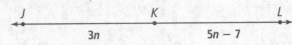

a. If JL = 25, what is n?   b. What is JK? KL?

HABITS OF MIND

Construct Arguments Gina says that for any segment $\overline{AB}$ on a number line, $AB = BA$. Do you agree? Explain. © MP.3

EXAMPLE 4

Try It! Use the Protractor Postulate to Measure an Angle

4. Refer to the figure.

   a. What is $m\angle AEC$?   b. What is $m\angle BED$?

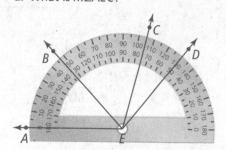

EXAMPLE 5

Try It! Use the Angle Addition Postulate to Solve Problems

5. Can the lighting designer use a spotlight with a 33° beam angle that can rotate 25° to the left and right to light all of the objects on the stage?

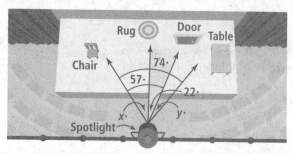

HABITS OF MIND

Use Appropriate Tools If M is a point in the interior of $\angle ABC$, would it be helpful to use a diagram to compare $m\angle ABM$ to $m\angle ABC$? Explain. © MP.5

Do You UNDERSTAND?

1.  **ESSENTIAL QUESTION** How are the properties of segments and angles used to determine their measures?

2. **Error Analysis** Ella wrote $AB = |-1 + 5| = 4$. Explain Ella's error. © **MP.3**

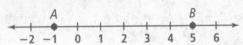

3. **Vocabulary** What does it mean for segments to be congruent? What does it mean for angles to be congruent?

4. **Make Sense and Persevere** Suppose M is a point in the interior of $\angle JKL$. If $m\angle MKL = 42$ and $m\angle JKL = 84$, what is $m\angle JKM$? © **MP.1**

Do You KNOW HOW?

Find the length of each segment.

5. $\overline{WX}$

6. $\overline{WY}$

7. Points A, B, and C are collinear and B is between A and C. Given $AB = 12$ and $AC = 19$, what is BC?

8. Given $m\angle JML = 80$ and $m\angle KML = 33$, what is $m\angle JMK$?

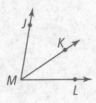

EXPLORE & REASON

Using a compass, make a design using only circles like the one shown.

A. What instructions can you give to another student so they can make a copy of your design?

B. Make Sense and Persevere Use a ruler to draw straight line segments to connect points where the circles intersect. Are any of the segments that you drew the same length? If so, why do you think they are? Ⓒ MP.1

HABITS OF MIND

Communicate Precisely What mathematical terms or concepts can you use to describe your design? Ⓒ MP.6

EXAMPLE 1

Try It! Use Congruent Angles and Congruent Segments

1. a. If $m\angle NOP = 2x + 2$, $m\angle POR = 3x - 5$, and $m\angle NOQ = 114$, what is the value of x?

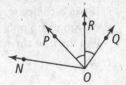

b. In the figure at the right, suppose $CD = 11.5$ cm, $DE = 5.3$ cm, and the perimeter of the figure is 73.8 cm. What is GE?

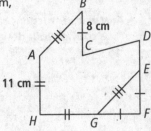

EXAMPLE 2

Try It! Copy a Segment

2. How can you construct a copy of $\overline{XY}$?

EXAMPLE 3

Try It! Copy an Angle

3. How can you construct a copy of $\angle B$?

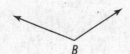

HABITS OF MIND

Construct Arguments Leo says a copy of a segment or angle is always congruent to the original, even if the orientation of the copy is different from the orientation of the original. Construct an argument to support or refute Leo's statement. Ⓒ **MP.3**

EXAMPLE 4

Try It! Construct an Angle Bisector

4. How can you construct the angle bisector of ∠G?

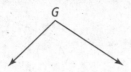

EXAMPLE 5

Try It! Use Constructions

5. The illustration shows three sculptures in the lobby of an art gallery. A new sculpture will be added to the lobby. Draw the line on which the new sculpture should be placed if it is to lie along the angle bisector of the angle formed by the three original sculptures.

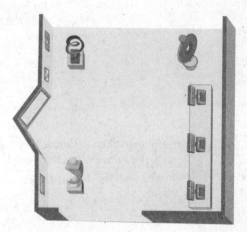

HABITS OF MIND

Look for Relationships How is constructing a copy of an angle like constructing an angle bisector? Ⓒ **MP.7**

Do You UNDERSTAND?

1. **ESSENTIAL QUESTION** How are a straightedge and compass used to make basic constructions?

Error Analysis Kanesha tries to copy ∠T but is unable to make an exact copy. Explain her error. © MP.3

2. **Vocabulary** When an angle bisector is drawn, what is the relationship between the two resulting angles?

Look for Relationships Diego is copying △ABC. First, he constructs $\overline{DE}$ as a copy of $\overline{AB}$. Next, he constructs ∠D as a copy of ∠A, using $\overline{DE}$ as one of the sides. Explain what he needs to do to complete the copy of the triangle. © MP.7

Do You KNOW HOW?

Construct a copy of each segment.

3.

4.
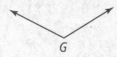

Construct a copy of each angle, and then construct its bisector.

5.
6.
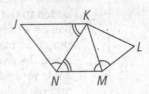

7. **Look for Relationships** In the diagram at the right, $m\angle LMN = 116$, $m\angle JKM = 122$, and $m\angle JNM = 103$. What is $m\angle NKM$? © MP.7

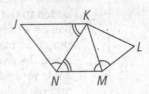

MODEL & SOLVE

LaTanya is decorating her living room and draws a floor plan to help look at placement.

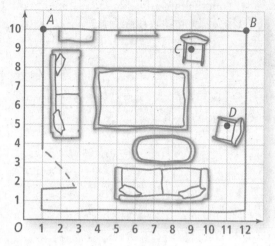

A. LaTanya wants to center a picture along the back wall. How do you find the point at the center between *A* and *B*?

B. Communicate Precisely LaTanya wants to place a lamp halfway between the chairs at points C and D. How can you find the point where the lamp should go? © MP.6

HABITS OF MIND

Use Appropriate Tools What tools did you use to help you answer the questions? Why was it helpful to use the tools you did? © MP.5

EXAMPLE 1

Try It! Find a Midpoint

1. Find the midpoint for each segment with the given endpoints.

   a. $C(-2, 5)$ and $D(8, -12)$

   b. $E(2.5, -7)$ and $F(-6.2, -3.8)$

EXAMPLE 2

Try It! Partition a Segment

2. Find the coordinates of each point described.

   a. $\overline{AB}$ in the ratio 7:3.

   b. $\frac{4}{5}$ of the way from B to A.

HABITS OF MIND

Generalize Is there a mathematical rule for finding the coordinates of the point R that is fraction q of the way from point $P(x_1, y_1)$ to $Q(x_2, y_2)$? Explain. © MP.8

EXAMPLE 3

Try It! Derive the Distance Formula

3. Tavon claims that $d \doteq \sqrt{(x_1 - x_2)^2 + (y_1 - y_2)^2}$ can also be used to find distance between two points. Is he correct? Explain.

EXAMPLE 4

Try It! Find the Distance

4. How far does the shortstop need to throw the ball to reach the first baseman? Round to the nearest tenth of a foot.

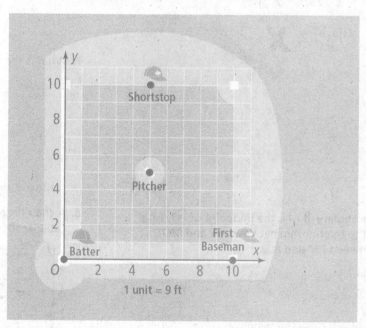

1 unit = 9 ft

HABITS OF MIND

Look for Relationships How do you relate the distance formula between two points to the Pythagorean Theorem? ⓒ **MP.7**

Do You UNDERSTAND?

1. **ESSENTIAL QUESTION** How are the midpoint and length of a segment on the coordinate plane determined?

2. **Error Analysis** Kaleel calculated the midpoint of $\overline{AB}$ with $A(-3, 5)$ and $B(1, 7)$. What is Kaleel's error? © **MP.3**

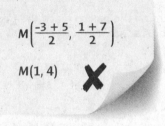

$$M\left(\frac{-3+5}{2}, \frac{1+7}{2}\right)$$

$$M(1, 4) \quad \times$$

3. **Vocabulary** If M is the midpoint of $\overline{PQ}$, what is the relationship between PM and MQ? Between PM and PQ?

4. **Reason** Is it possible for $\overline{PQ}$ to have two distinct midpoints, $M_1(a, b)$ and $M_2(c, d)$? Explain. © **MP.2**

Do You KNOW HOW?

$\overline{PQ}$ has endpoints at $P(-5, 4)$ and $Q(7, -5)$.

5. What is the midpoint of $\overline{PQ}$?

6. What are the coordinates of the point $\frac{2}{3}$ of the way from P to Q?

7. What is the length of $\overline{PQ}$?

8. A chair lift at a ski resort travels along the cable as shown.

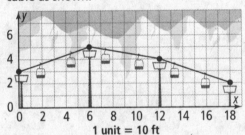

1 unit = 10 ft

How long is the cable? Round your answer to the nearest whole foot.

EXPLORE & REASON

When points on a circle are connected, the line segments divide the circle into a number of regions, as shown.

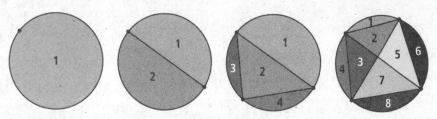

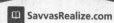
A. How does the number of regions change when another point is added?

B. Look for Relationships Using the pattern you observed, make a prediction about the number of regions formed by connecting 5 points on a circle. Make a drawing to test your prediction. Is your prediction correct? Ⓒ MP.7

HABITS OF MIND

Generalize Does an observation of a pattern always prove a relationship? Explain. Ⓒ MP.8

EXAMPLE 1

Try It! Use Inductive Reasoning to Extend a Pattern

1. What appear to be the next two terms in each sequence?

a. 800, 400, 200, 100,...   b. 18, 24, 32, $\frac{128}{3}$,...

EXAMPLE 2

Try It! Use Inductive Reasoning to Make a Conjecture

2. a. How many dots are in the 5th and 6th terms of the pattern?

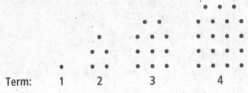

Term: 1   2   3   4

b. What conjecture can you make about the number of dots in the nth term of the pattern?

EXAMPLE 3

Try It! Use a Conjecture to Make a Prediction

3. Based on the data, about how many members would you expect the chess club to have in its 5th year?

Year	1	2	3	4
Club Members	10	13	17	22

HABITS OF MIND

Look for Relationships What strategies can you use to find patterns in numbers presented in a sequence or in a table? What strategies can you use to find patterns with dots or other visual patterns? © **MP.7**

EXAMPLE 4

Try It! Find a Counterexample to Show a Conjecture is False

4. What is a counterexample that shows the statement, *the sum of two composite numbers must be a composite number*, is false?

EXAMPLE 5

Try It! Test a Conjecture

5. For each conjecture, test the conjecture with several more examples or find a counterexample to disprove it.

  a. For every integer *n*, the value of n^2 is positive.

  b. A number is divisible by 4 if the last two digits are divisible by 4.

HABITS OF MIND

Construct Arguments Tyler says that only one example is needed to prove that a conjecture is true. Do you agree? ⓒ MP.3

Do You UNDERSTAND?

1. **ESSENTIAL QUESTION** How is inductive reasoning used to recognize mathematical relationships?

2. **Error Analysis** Esteban made the following drawing and then stated this conjecture: "The altitude of a triangle always lies inside of or along the side of the triangle." What error did Esteban make? © **MP.3**

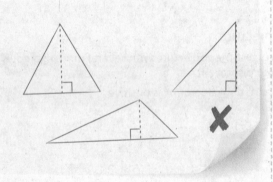

3. **Vocabulary** What type of statement results from inductive reasoning?

Do You KNOW HOW?

4. What appear to be the next three numbers in the pattern?

    4, 11, 18, 25,...

5. What conjecture can you make about the number of regions created by *n* unique diameters?

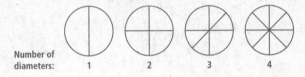

Number of diameters: 1 2 3 4

6. Can you find four examples that are true or a counterexample for the following statement?

    For every integer *n*, the value of $n^2 + 1$ is odd.

The Mystery Spokes

Some photos are taken in such a way that it is difficult to determine exactly what the picture shows. Sometimes it's because the photo is a close up part of an object, and you do not see the entire object. Other times, it might be because the photographer used special effects when taking the photo.

You can often use clues from the photo to determine what is in the photo and also what the rest of the object might look like. What clues would you look for? Think about this during the Mathematical Modeling in 3 Acts lesson.

SavvasRealize.com

ACT 1 Identify the Problem

1. What is the first question that comes to mind after watching the video?

2. Write down the main question you will answer.

3. Make an initial conjecture that answers this main question.

4. Explain how you arrived at your conjecture.

5. Write a number that you know is too small.

6. Write a number that you know is too large.

ACT 2 ▶ Develop a Model

7. Use the math that you have learned in this Topic to refine your conjecture.

ACT 3 ▶ Interpret the Results

8. Is your refined conjecture between the highs and lows you set up earlier?

9. Did your refined conjecture match the actual answer exactly? If not, what might explain the difference?

EXPLORE & REASON

If-then statements show a cause and effect. The table shows some if-then statements.

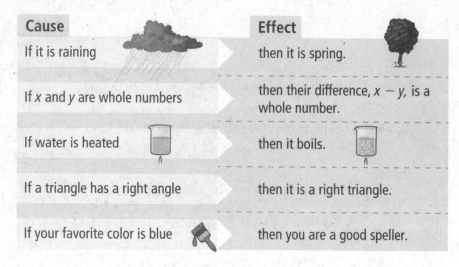

Cause	Effect
If it is raining	then it is spring.
If x and y are whole numbers	then their difference, $x - y$, is a whole number.
If water is heated	then it boils.
If a triangle has a right angle	then it is a right triangle.
If your favorite color is blue	then you are a good speller.

A. Construct Arguments Determine whether each effect is always true for the given cause, or is not necessarily true for the given cause. For the effects that are not necessarily true, how could you change them to make them always true? ©MP.3

B. Write some if-then statements of your own. Write two statements that are always true and two statements that are not necessarily true.

HABITS OF MIND

Look for Relationships You have used the words *hypothesis* and *conclusion* in other classes. How are their meanings the same as or different from the definitions in geometry? ©MP.7

EXAMPLE 1

Try It! Write a Conditional Statement

1. Write each statement as a conditional.

    a. A triangle with all angles congruent is equilateral.

    b. Alberto can go to the movies if he washes the car.

EXAMPLE 2

Try It! Find a Truth Value of a Conditional

2. What is the truth value of each conditional? Explain your reasoning.

    a. If a quadrilateral has a right angle, then it is a rectangle.

    b. If X is the midpoint of $\overline{AB}$, then X lies on $\overline{AB}$.

EXAMPLE 3

Try It! Write and Evaluate the Truth Value of a Converse

3. Write and determine the truth value of the converse of the conditional.

    a. If a polygon is a quadrilateral, then it has four sides.

    b. If two angles are complementary, then their angle measures add to 90.

EXAMPLE 4

Try It! Write and Evaluate the Truth Value of an Inverse and a Contrapositive

4. Write the converse, the inverse, and the contrapositive. What is the truth value of each?

   If today is a weekend day, then tomorrow is Monday.

HABITS OF MIND

Reason What is the truth value of the conditional, "If 11 is an even number, then there are 23 hours in a day?" What are the truth values of the hypothesis and conclusion? Is this true of all conditionals where the hypothesis can never be true? Ⓒ MP.2

EXAMPLE 5

Try It! Write and Evaluate a Biconditional

5. Write a biconditional for the following conditional. What is its truth value?

   If two lines intersect at right angles, then they are perpendicular.

EXAMPLE 6

Try It! Identify the Conditionals in a Biconditional

6. What are the two conditionals associated with the biconditional?

   The product of two numbers is negative if and only if the numbers have opposite signs.

HABITS OF MIND

Generalize How is a biconditional similar to giving a definition? Can you think of a definition in geometry and express it as a biconditional? Ⓒ MP.8

Do You UNDERSTAND?

1. **ESSENTIAL QUESTION** How do if-then statements describe mathematical relationships?

2. **Error Analysis** Alma was asked to write the inverse of the following conditional.

   If it is sunny, then I use sunscreen.

   What error did Alma make? © MP.3

   If it is not sunny, then I use sunscreen.

   ✗

3. **Vocabulary** Which term is used to describe the opposite of a statement?

4. **Generalize** How do you write the converse of a conditional? How do you write the contrapositive of a conditional? © MP.8

5. **Communicate Precisely** Explain how the inverse and the contrapositive of a conditional are alike and how they are different. © MP.6

Do You KNOW HOW?

6. Write the following statement as a biconditional.

   A prime number has only 1 and itself as factors.

For Exercises 7–9, use the following conditional.

   If a rectangle has an area of 12 m², then it has sides of length 3 m and 4 m.

7. What is the hypothesis? What is the conclusion?

8. What is the truth value of the conditional? What would be a counterexample?

9. What are the converse, the inverse, and the contrapositive? What are their truth values?

10. What two conditionals are implied by the following biconditional?

    "The city can build new roads if and only if the sales tax is raised to 8%."

CRITIQUE & EXPLAIN

A deck of 60 game cards are numbered from 1 to 15 on one of four different shapes (triangle, circle, square, and pentagon). A teacher selects five cards and displays four of the cards.

She tells her class that all of the cards she selected have the same shape and asks them to draw a conclusion about the fifth card.

Chen

The fifth card is 11.

Carolina

The fifth card has a circle.

A. Describe how each student might have reached his or her conclusion. Is each student's conclusion valid? Explain.

B. Make Sense and Persevere What are other possibilities of the fifth card? What could the teacher say to narrow the possibilities? © **MP.1**

HABITS OF MIND

Make Sense and Persevere How else might you represent the situation? © **MP.1**

EXAMPLE 1

Try It! **Determine Whether a Statement Is True**

1. Given that a conditional and its hypothesis are true, can you determine whether the conclusion is true?

EXAMPLE 2

Try It! **Apply the Law of Detachment to Draw Real-World and Mathematical Conclusions**

2. Assume that each set of given information is true.

 a. If two angles are congruent, then the measures of the two angles are equal to each other. Angle 1 is congruent to ∠2. What can you logically conclude about the measures of ∠1 and ∠2?

 b. If you finish the race in under 30 minutes, then you win a prize. You finished the race in 26 minutes. What can you logically conclude?

HABITS OF MIND

Generalize In part (a), what would happen if ∠1 were not congruent to ∠2? © MP.8

EXAMPLE 3

Try It! Apply the Law of Syllogism to Draw Real-World and Mathematical Conclusions

3. Assume that each set of conditionals is true. Use the Law of Syllogism to draw a conclusion.

   a. If an integer is divisible by 6, it is divisible by 2. If an integer is divisible by 2, then it is an even number.

   b. If it is a holiday, then you don't have to go to school. If it is Labor Day, then it is a holiday.

EXAMPLE 4

Try It! Apply the Laws of Detachment and Syllogism to Draw Conclusions

4. If a quadrilateral has four right angles, then it is a rectangle. If a quadrilateral is a rectangle, then it has two sets of parallel sides.

   A polygon has four sides and four right angles. Using the Law of Detachment and the Law of Syllogism, what conclusion can you draw?

HABITS OF MIND

Construct Arguments Compare the situations in Examples 3 and 4. What is the same about them? What is different? © MP.3

EXAMPLE 5

Try It! Use Geometric Definitions and Mathematical Properties to Draw Conclusions

5. Suppose point D is in the interior of $\angle ABC$. Use deductive reasoning to draw a conclusion about $m\angle DBC$.

Do You UNDERSTAND?

1. **ESSENTIAL QUESTION** How can you use given and previously known facts to draw conclusions?

2. **Error Analysis** Dakota writes the following as an example of using the Law of Detachment. What is her error? © MP.3

> If my favorite team wins more than 55 games, they win the championship. My team won the championship, so they won more than 55 games. ✗

3. **Vocabulary** What are the differences between the Law of Detachment and the Law of Syllogism?

4. **Use Structure** How can representing sentences and phrases with symbols help you determine whether to apply the Law of Detachment or the Law of Syllogism? © MP.7

Do You KNOW HOW?

Assume that each set of given information is true.

5. If you have a temperature above 100.4°F, then you have a fever. Mario has a temperature of 101.2°F. What can you conclude about Mario? What rule of inference did you use?

6. If points A, B, and C are collinear with B between A and C, then $AB + BC = AC$. Use the information in the figure shown. What can you conclude about AC?

```
        3x        5x − 3
  ◄──●─────────●───────────●──►
     A         B           C
```

Assume that each set of conditionals is true. Use the Law of Syllogism to write a true conditional.

7. If you eat too much, you get a stomach ache. If you get a stomach ache, you want to rest.

8. If two numbers are odd, the sum of the numbers is even. If a number is even, then the number is divisible by 2.

CRITIQUE & EXPLAIN

William solved an equation for *x* and wrote justifications for each step of his solution.

$6(14 + x) = 108$	Given
$84 + 6x = 108$	Distributive Property
$6x = 108 - 84$	Subtraction Property of Equality
$6x = 24$	Simplify
$x = 4$	Multiplication Property of Equality

A. Make Sense and Persevere Are William's justifications valid at each step? If not, what might you change? Explain. © **MP.1**

B. Can you justify another series of steps that result in the same solution for *x*?

HABITS OF MIND

Use Structure What ideas have you learned before that were useful in evaluating William's solution? © **MP.7**

EXAMPLE 1

Try It! Write a Two-Column Proof

1. Write a two-column proof.

   Given: $\overrightarrow{BD}$ bisects $\angle CBE$.

   Prove: $\angle ABD \cong \angle FBD$

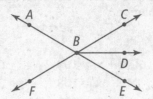

HABITS OF MIND

Use Appropriate Tools What do you know that is not stated in the problem? ⓒ MP.5

EXAMPLE 2

Try It! Apply the Vertical Angles Theorem

2. Find the value of x and the measure of each labeled angle.

a.

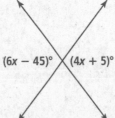

b.

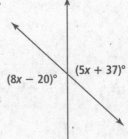

HABITS OF MIND

Communicate Precisely What steps can you take to verify that each solution is correct? ⓒ MP.6

EXAMPLE 3

Try It! Write a Paragraph Proof

3. Write a paragraph proof of the Congruent Complements Theorem.

   Given: ∠1 and ∠2 are complementary.
   ∠2 and ∠3 are complementary.

   Prove: ∠1 ≅ ∠3

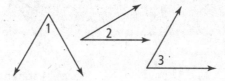

EXAMPLE 4

Try It! Write a Proof Using a Theorem

4. Write a two-column proof.

   Given: $m\angle 4 = 35$, $m\angle 1 = m\angle 2 + m\angle 4$

   Prove: $m\angle 3 = 70$

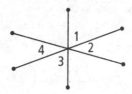

HABITS OF MIND

Reason What properties, theorems, or definitions did you use to prove $m\angle 3 = 70$? © MP.2

Do You UNDERSTAND?

1. **ESSENTIAL QUESTION** How is deductive reasoning used to prove a theorem?

2. **Error Analysis** Jayden states that based on the Congruent Supplements Theorem, if $m\angle 1 + m\angle 2 = 90$ and if $m\angle 1 + m\angle 3 = 90$, then $\angle 2 \cong \angle 3$. What is the error in Jayden's reasoning? © MP.3

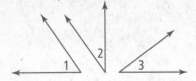

3. **Vocabulary** How is a theorem different from a postulate? How is a theorem different from a conjecture?

4. **Reason** If $\angle 2$ and $\angle 3$ are complementary, how could you use the Vertical Angles Theorem to find $m\angle 1$? © MP.2

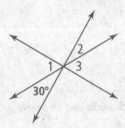

Do You KNOW HOW?

Use the figures to answer Exercises 5–7.

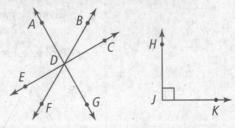

5. What statement could you write in a proof for $m\angle ADC$ using the Angle Addition Postulate as a reason?

6. Could you use the Vertical Angles Theorem as a reason in a proof to state $m\angle ADC = m\angle EDG$ or to state $\angle ADC \cong \angle EDG$? Explain.

7. Given $m\angle ADC = 90$, what reason could you give in a proof to state $\angle ADC \cong \angle HJK$?

8. The Tower of Pisa, in Italy, began tilting during its construction in the 12th century. It currently leans at an angle of about 4° from the vertical, as shown. What equation for the measure of x, the angle it makes from the horizontal, could you use in a proof?

CRITIQUE & EXPLAIN

Philip presents the following number puzzle to his friends.

The number is a prime number. The square of the number is less than 100 and greater than 10. The number is not a factor of 21. What is the number?

A. Make Sense and Persevere Philip states that the number must be 7. Explain why this cannot be true. ⓒ **MP.1**

B. Write your own number puzzle that has an answer of 5. Your friend says the answer is not 5. How do you use the statements of your puzzle to identify the contradiction?

HABITS OF MIND

Communicate Precisely For Part B, explain how you might show that your solution is the answer to the number puzzle. ⓒ **MP.6**

EXAMPLE 1

Try It! Use Assumptions to Draw a Conclusion

1. Draw a conclusion in the following situation.

   A bagel shop gives customers a free bagel on their birthday. Thato went to the bagel shop today but did not get a free bagel.

EXAMPLE 2

Try It! Write an Indirect Proof by Contradiction

2. Write an indirect proof for the statement using proof by contradiction.

   If $\angle A$ and $\angle B$ are complementary, then $m\angle A < 90$.

EXAMPLE 3

Try It! Write an Indirect Proof by Contrapositive

3. Write an indirect proof of each statement using proof by contrapositive.

a. If a number is an integer, it is rational.

b. If a whole number is between 1 and 4, it is a factor of 6.

HABITS OF MIND

Generalize Will the strategy you used to prove each statement work in proving other conditional statements? © MP.8

Do You UNDERSTAND?

1. **ESSENTIAL QUESTION** What can you conclude when valid reasoning leads to a contradiction?

2. **Vocabulary** What are the two types of indirect proof? How are they similar and how are they different?

3. **Error Analysis** Consider the figure below.

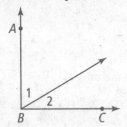

Consider the following conditional.

If ∠ABC is a right angle and $m\angle 1 < 60$, then $m\angle 2 > 30$.

A student will prove the contrapositive as a way of proving the conditional. The student plans to assume $m\angle 2 < 30$ and then prove $m\angle 1 > 60$. Explain the error in the student's plan. © MP.3

4. **Make Sense and Persevere** How do truth tables explain why proving the contrapositive also proves the original conditional statement? © MP.1

5. **Generalize** Explain how you can identify the statement you assume and the statement you try to prove when writing a proof by contrapositive. © MP.8

Do You KNOW HOW?

Use indirect reasoning to draw a conclusion in each situation.

6. Tamira only cuts the grass on a day that it does not rain. She cut the grass on Thursday.

7. Gabriela works at the library every Saturday morning. She did not work at the library this morning.

Write the first step of an indirect proof for each of the following statements.

8. $m\angle JKM = m\angle JKL - m\angle MKL$

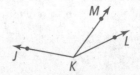

9. $\overline{PQ}$ is perpendicular to $\overline{ST}$.

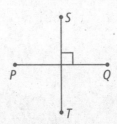

10. What can you conclude from the following situation using indirect reasoning? Explain.

   • Nadeem spent more than $10 but less than $11 for a sandwich and drink.

   • He spent $8.49 on his sandwich.

   • The cost for milk is $1.49.

   • The cost for orange juice is $2.49.

   • The cost for a tropical smoothie is $2.89.

   • The cost for apple juice is $2.59.

EXPLORE & REASON

The diagram shows two parallel lines
cut by a transversal.

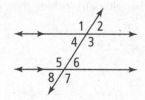

A. Look for Relationships What relationships among the measures of the angles
do you see? ⓒ MP.7

B. Suppose a different transversal intersects the parallel lines. Would
you expect to find the same relationships with the measures of
those angles? Explain.

HABITS OF MIND

Look for Relationships What theorems have you already learned that can be used
to show why some of the angles formed are congruent? ⓒ MP.7

EXAMPLE 1

Try It! Identify Angle Pairs

1. Which angle pairs include the named angle?

   a. ∠4   b. ∠7

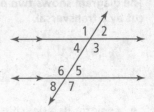

EXAMPLE 2

Try It! Explore Angle Relationships

2. For parts a and b, use the figure to the right.

   a. If $m\angle 4 = 118$, what is the measure of each of the other angles?

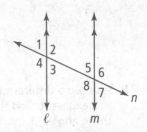

   b. If $m\angle 2 = 9x - 12$ and $m\angle 4 = 6x + 30$, what is $m\angle 5$?

EXAMPLE 3

Try It! Prove the Alternate Interior Angles Theorem

3. Prove the Corresponding Angles Theorem.

   Given: $m \parallel n$

   Prove: $\angle 1 \cong \angle 2$

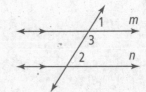

- -

HABITS OF MIND

Generalize Suppose that a transversal intersects a pair of parallel lines, and one of the interior angles created measures x. What must be true of the other interior angles created? ⓒ **MP.8**

EXAMPLE 4

Try It! Use Parallel Lines to Prove an Angle Relationship

4. Given $\overline{AB} \parallel \overline{CD}$, prove that $m\angle 1 + m\angle 2 + m\angle 3 = 180$.

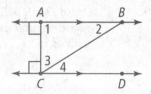

EXAMPLE 5

Try It! Find Angle Measures

5. In the diagram, $\overline{AC} \parallel \overline{EG}$, $\overline{JA} \parallel \overline{HB}$, and $\overline{JC} \parallel \overline{KG}$. If $m\angle EJF = 56$, find $m\angle FHK$.

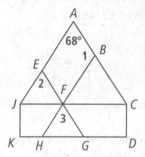

HABITS OF MIND

Make Sense and Persevere What are some strategies you can use to find unknown angle measures? © MP.1

Do You UNDERSTAND?

1. **ESSENTIAL QUESTION** What angle relationships are created when parallel lines are intersected by a transversal?

2. **Vocabulary** When a transversal intersects two parallel lines, which angle pairs are congruent?

3. **Error Analysis** What error did Leah make? © MP.3

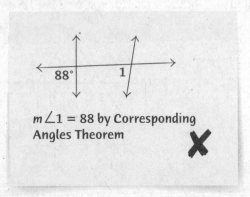

$m\angle 1 = 88$ by Corresponding Angles Theorem

4. **Generalize** For any pair of angles formed by a transversal intersecting parallel lines, what are two possible relationships? © MP.8

Do You KNOW HOW?

Use the diagram for Exercises 5–10.

Classify each pair of angles. Compare angle measures, and give the postulate or theorem that justifies it.

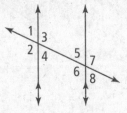

5. $\angle 2$ and $\angle 6$

6. $\angle 3$ and $\angle 5$

If $m\angle 1 = 71$, find the measure of each angle.

7. $\angle 5$

8. $\angle 7$

If $m\angle 3 = 3x + 12$ and $m\angle 5 = 2x + 3$, find the measure of each angle.

9. $\angle 5$ 10. $\angle 7$

11. Elm St. and Spruce St. are parallel. What is $m\angle 1$?

CRITIQUE & EXPLAIN

Juan analyzes the diagram to see if line ℓ is parallel to line m. His teacher asks if there is enough information to say whether the lines are parallel.

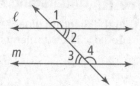

> Yes, if a transversal intersects two parallel lines, then alternate interior angles are congruent and corresponding angles are congruent. I have both angle relationships here, so the lines are parallel.

A. Make Sense and Persevere Why is Juan's statement correct or incorrect? Ⓒ **MP.1**

B. Can you use the Alternate Exterior Angles Theorem to prove that the lines are not parallel?

HABITS OF MIND

Make Sense and Persevere Would Juan's statement be correct if he had referred to same-side interior angles instead of corresponding angles or alternate interior angles? Explain. Ⓒ **MP.1**

EXAMPLE 1

Try It! Understand Angle Relationships

1. In the diagram, lines ℓ and m are parallel, but lines t and m are not parallel. Could ∠3 be supplementary to a 120° angle? Explain.

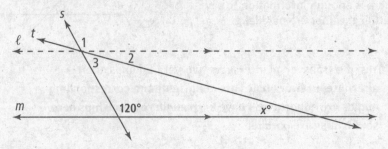

EXAMPLE 2

Try It! Write a Flow Proof of Theorem 2-5

2. Write a flow proof for Theorem 2-6, the Converse of the Same-Side Interior Angles Postulate.

HABITS OF MIND

Construct Arguments How do you decide which statements to start with when writing a flow proof? © MP.3

EXAMPLE 3

Try It! Determine Whether Lines Are Parallel

3. What should ∠4 and ∠5 measure to ensure that the right edges of the trapezoids in the diagram are parallel to each other?

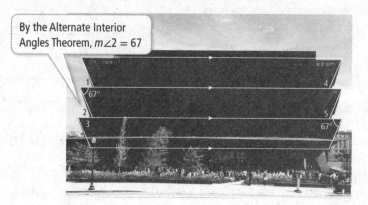

By the Alternate Interior Angles Theorem, $m\angle 2 = 67$

EXAMPLE 4

Try It! Construct a Parallel Line

4. Construct a line parallel to the given line through point P.

P

EXAMPLE 5

Try It! Solve a Problem With Parallel Lines

5. a. In the illustration, boards *v* and *w* are parallel. Bailey needs board *c* to be parallel to board *a*. What should ∠2 measure? Explain.

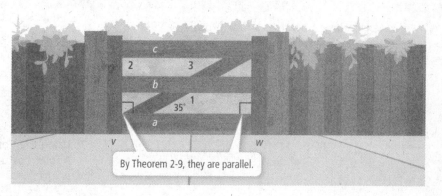

By Theorem 2-9, they are parallel.

   b. Is *b* ∥ *c*? Explain.

- -

HABITS OF MIND

Make Sense and Persevere When using angles formed by a transversal to prove that two lines are parallel, how do you decide which pair of angles to use in your proof? Ⓒ **MP.1**

Do You UNDERSTAND?

1. **ESSENTIAL QUESTION** What angle relationships can be used to prove that two lines intersected by a transversal are parallel?

2. **Error Analysis** Noemi wrote, "If ∠1 ≅ ∠2, then by the Converse of the Same-Side Interior Angles Postulate, ℓ ∥ m." Explain the error in Noemi's reasoning. © **MP.3**

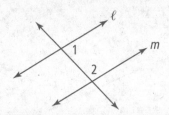

3. **Vocabulary** How does a *flow proof* show logical steps in the proof of a conditional statement?

4. **Reason** How is Theorem 2-9 a special case of the Converse of the Corresponding Angles Theorem? © **MP.2**

Do You KNOW HOW?

Use the figure shown for Exercises 5 and 6.

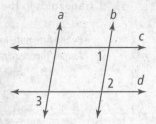

5. If ∠1 ≅ ∠2, which theorem proves that c ∥ d?

6. If $m\angle 2 = 4x - 6$ and $m\angle 3 = 2x + 18$, for what value of x is a ∥ b? Which theorem justifies your answer?

7. Using the Converse of the Same-Side Interior Angles Postulate, what equation shows that g ∥ h?

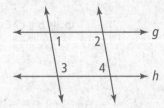

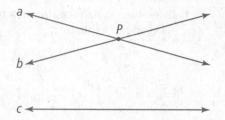
EXPLORE & REASON

Two parallel lines never intersect. But, can two lines that intersect ever be parallel to the same line?

Draw point *P*. Then draw lines *a* and *b* that intersect at point *P* as shown.

a

P

b

c

A. Place a pencil below the intersecting lines on your paper to represent line *c*. Rotate the pencil so that it is parallel to line *b*. Can you rotate the pencil so that it is parallel to line *a* at the same time as line *b*?

B. Look for Relationships Can you adjust your drawing of the two intersecting lines so you can rotate the pencil to be parallel to both lines? Ⓒ **MP.7**

HABITS OF MIND

Look for Relationships Suppose you draw two lines that are parallel. Is it possible to draw a third line that intersects only one of the parallel lines? Explain. Ⓒ **MP.7**

EXAMPLE 1

Try It! Investigate the Measures of Triangle Angles

1. Given two angle measures in a triangle, can you find the measure of the third angle? Explain.

EXAMPLE 2

Try It! Prove the Triangle Angle-Sum Theorem

2. How does Theorem 2-10 justify the construction of the line through C that is parallel to $\overleftrightarrow{AB}$?

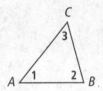

EXAMPLE 3

Try It! Use the Triangle Angle-Sum Theorem

3. What are the values of x and y in each figure?

a.

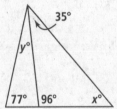

b.

42°   57°
x°
y°   59°

HABITS OF MIND

Reason When applying the Angle Sum Postulate in the Triangle Angle-Sum Theorem, how do you know that the sum of the angle measures is 180°? Ⓒ MP.2

EXAMPLE 4

Try It! Apply the Triangle Exterior Angle Theorem

4. What is the value of x in each figure?

a.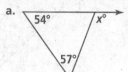

b.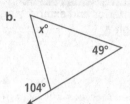

EXAMPLE 5

Try It! Apply the Triangle Theorems

5. In the figure, $m\angle 1 = m\angle 4$. What is $m\angle 5$? Explain.

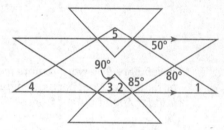

HABITS OF MIND

Look for Relationships How is the Triangle Exterior Angle Theorem related to the Triangle Angle-Sum Theorem? Ⓒ MP.7

Do You UNDERSTAND?

1. **ESSENTIAL QUESTION** What is true about the interior and exterior angle measures of any triangle?

2. **Error Analysis** Cheng determined that the value of *x* is 103 and the value of *y* is 132 in the figure below. What mistake did Cheng make? ⓒ **MP.3**

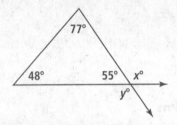

3. **Vocabulary** The word *remote* means distant or far apart. What parts of a figure are *remote interior angles* distant from?

4. **Look for Relationships** Use the Triangle Angle-Sum Theorem to answer the following questions. Explain your answers.

   a. What are the measures of each angle of an equiangular triangle?

   b. If one of the angle measures of an isosceles triangle is 90, what are the measures of the other two angles? ⓒ **MP.7**

Do You KNOW HOW?

What is the value of *x* in each figure?

5. 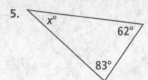 **6.**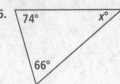

What is the value of *x* in each figure?

7. 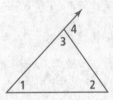 **8.**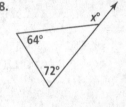

9. Write an equation relating the measures of ∠1, ∠2, and ∠3. Write another equation relating the measures of ∠1, ∠2, and ∠4.

MODEL & DISCUSS

Pilar and Jake begin climbing to the top of a 100-ft monument at the same time along two different sets of steps at the same rate. The tables show their distances above ground level after a number of steps.

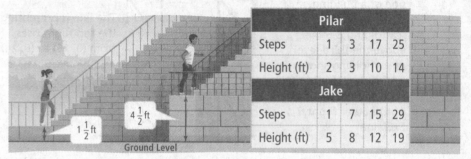

Pilar				
Steps	1	3	17	25
Height (ft)	2	3	10	14
Jake				
Steps	1	7	15	29
Height (ft)	5	8	12	19

$1\frac{1}{2}$ ft $4\frac{1}{2}$ ft Ground Level

A. How many feet does each student climb after 10 steps? Explain.

B. Will Pilar and Jake be at the same height after the same number of steps? Explain.

C. Reason What would you expect the graphs of each to look like given your answers to parts A and B? Explain. Ⓒ MP.2

HABITS OF MIND

Reason What would it mean if the graphs intersected? Ⓒ MP.2

EXAMPLE 1

Try It! Slopes of Parallel Lines

1. The diagrams represent three levels of scaffolding on the side of a building. A fourth level of scaffolding is 6 feet above the third level of scaffolding shown. Is the fourth flight of stairs parallel to any of the other flights? Explain.

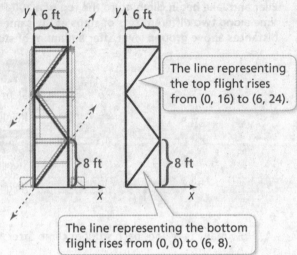

The line representing the top flight rises from (0, 16) to (6, 24).

The line representing the bottom flight rises from (0, 0) to (6, 8).

EXAMPLE 2

Try It! Check Parallelism

2. Are lines m and q in the graph parallel?

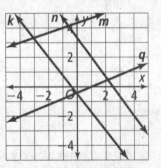

- -

HABITS OF MIND

Reason Could two lines that are parallel ever pass through the same point? © MP.2

EXAMPLE 3

Try It! Check Perpendicularity

3. a. Are lines *h* and *ℓ* in the diagram
perpendicular?

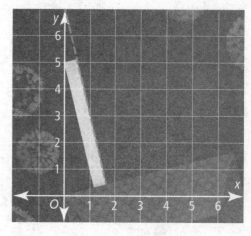

  b. Are lines *k* and *m* perpendicular?

EXAMPLE 4

Try It! Write Equations of Parallel and Perpendicular Lines

4. What are equations of lines parallel and perpendicular to the given line
passing through point *T*?

  a. $y = -3x + 2$; $T(3, 1)$

  b. $y = \frac{3}{4}x - 5$; $T(12, -2)$

EXAMPLE 5

Try It! Use Slope to Solve a Problem

5. The landscaping plans show
a sidewalk leading from the
back of a house to where a
shed will be built. The line
representing the edge of the
roof has a slope of $\frac{1}{4}$. The
landscape architect wants the
front of the shed to be parallel
to the back of the house. If
one corner of the shed is at
(0, 5), can the other corner be
at (3, 6.5)? Explain.

HABITS OF MIND

Generalize How can you use slope to determine if two lines are
perpendicular, parallel, or neither perpendicular nor parallel? © MP.8

Do You UNDERSTAND?

1. **ESSENTIAL QUESTION** How do the slopes of the lines that are parallel to each other compare? How do the slopes of lines that are perpendicular to each other compare?

2. **Error Analysis** Katrina said that the lines $y = -\frac{2}{3}x + 5$ and $y = -\frac{3}{2}x + 2$ are perpendicular. Explain Katrina's error. © **MP.3**

3. **Reason** Give an equation for a line perpendicular to the line $y = 0$. Is there more than one such line? Explain. © **MP.2**

4. **Communicate Precisely** What are two different if-then statements implied by Theorem 2-13? © **MP.6**

5. **Error Analysis** Duante said that $\overleftrightarrow{AB}$ and $\overleftrightarrow{CD}$ for $A(-2, 0)$, $B(2, 3)$, $C(1, -1)$, and $D(5, -4)$ are parallel. Explain and correct Duante's error. © **MP.3**

> slope of $\overleftrightarrow{AB}$: $\dfrac{3 - 0}{2 - (-2)} = \dfrac{3}{4}$
>
> slope of $\overleftrightarrow{CD}$: $\dfrac{-1 - (-4)}{5 - 1} = \dfrac{3}{4}$
>
> slopes are equal, so $\overleftrightarrow{AB} \parallel \overleftrightarrow{CD}$

Do You KNOW HOW?

Use the diagram for Exercises 6–9.

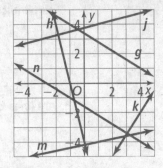

6. Are lines g and n parallel?

7. Are lines j and m parallel?

8. Are lines n and k perpendicular?

9. Are lines h and j perpendicular?

10. What is an equation for the line parallel to $y = -x + 7$ that passes through $(7, -2)$?

11. What is an equation for the line perpendicular to $y = 3x - 1$ that passes through $(-9, -2)$?

12. The graph of a roller coaster track goes in a straight line through coordinates $(10, 54)$ and $(42, 48)$, with coordinates in feet. A support beam runs parallel 12 feet below the track. What equation describes the support beam?

Parallel Paving Company

Building roads consists of many different tasks. Once civil engineers have designed the road, they work with surveyors and construction crews to clear and level the land. Sometimes specialists have to blast away rock in order to clear the land. Once the land is leveled, the crews bring in asphalt pavers to smooth out the hot asphalt.

Sometimes construction crews will start work at both ends of the new road and meet in the middle. Think about this during the Mathematical Modeling in 3 Acts lesson.

MATHEMATICAL MODELING IN **3** ACTS

SavvasRealize.com

SavvasRealize.com

ACT 1 ▶ **Identify the Problem**

1. What is the first question that comes to mind after watching the video?

2. Write down the main question you will answer.

3. Make an initial conjecture that answers this main question.

4. Explain how you arrived at your conjecture.

5. What information will be useful to know to answer the main question? How can you get it? How will you use that information?

ACT 2 ▶ Develop a Model

6. Use the math that you have learned in the topic to refine your conjecture.

ACT 3 ▶ Interpret the Results

7. Did your refined conjecture match the actual answer exactly? If not, what might explain the difference?

EXPLORE & REASON

The illustration shows irregular pentagon-shaped tiles covering a floor.

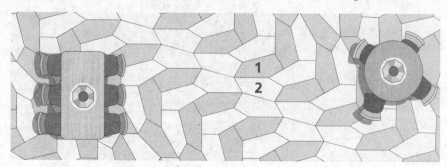

A. Which tiles are copies of tile 1? Explain.

B. **Communicate Precisely** If you were to move tile 1 from the design, what actions would you have to do so it completely covers tile 2? Ⓒ **MP.6**

C. Which tiles are *not* copies of tile 1? Explain.

HABITS OF MIND

Use Structure What patterns do you see in how the tiles cover the floor? Ⓒ **MP.7**

EXAMPLE 1

Try It! Identify Rigid Motions

1. Is each transformation a rigid motion? Explain.

a.

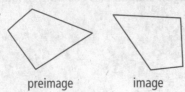

preimage   image

b.

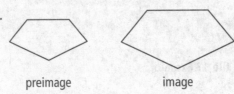

preimage   image

- -

HABITS OF MIND

Construct Arguments What kind of evidence would you give to show that a transformation is not a rigid motion? Ⓒ **MP.3**

EXAMPLE 2

Try It! Reflect a Triangle Across a Line

2. Sketch the reflection of △LMN across line n.

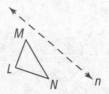

EXAMPLE 3

Try It! Reflect a Figure on a Coordinate Plane

3. Triangle ABC has vertices A(−5, 6), B(1, −2), and C(−3, −4). What are the coordinates of the vertices of △A′B′C′ for each reflection?

a. $r_{x\text{-axis}}$

b. reflection across the y-axis

EXAMPLE 4

Try It! Describe a Reflection on the Coordinate Plane

4. What is a reflection rule that maps each triangle to its image?

a. $C(3, 8)$, $D(5, 12)$, $E(4, 6)$ and $C'(-8, -3)$, $D'(-12, -5)$, $E'(-6, -4)$

b. $F(7, 6)$, $G(0, -4)$, $H(-5, 0)$ and $F'(-5, 6)$, $G'(2, -4)$, $H'(7, 0)$

HABITS OF MIND

Reason What is the relationship between a preimage point to the line of reflection and its image point to the line of reflection? © MP.2

EXAMPLE 5

Try It! Use Reflections

5. Student A sees the reflected image across the mirror of another student who appears to be at B'. Show the actual position of Student B.

B'
•

———————————————— mirror

•
A

HABITS OF MIND

Make Sense and Persevere What is the relationship between an image you see in a mirror and the actual image? © MP.1

Do You UNDERSTAND?

1. **ESSENTIAL QUESTION** How are the properties of reflection used to transform a figure?

2. **Error Analysis** Oscar drew the image of a triangle reflected across the line $y = -1$. What mistake did Oscar make? © MP.3

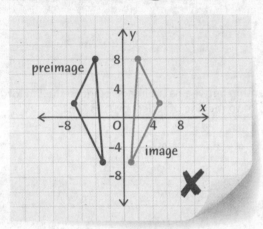

3. **Vocabulary** One meaning of the word *rigid* is "not bendable," and another is "unable to be changed." How do those meanings correspond to the definition of rigid motion?

4. **Communicate Precisely** How can you determine whether the transformation of a figure is a rigid motion? © MP.6

5. **Generalize** Describe the steps you must take to identify the path an object will follow if it bounces off a surface and strikes another object. © MP.8

Do You KNOW HOW?

6. Does the transformation shown appear to be a rigid motion? Explain.

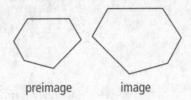

preimage   image

What are the coordinates of each image?

7. $r_{x\text{-axis}}(-5, 3)$

8. $r_{x\text{-axis}}(1, 6)$

9. Write a reflection rule that maps each triangle to its image.

   a. $J(1, 0)$, $K(-5, 2)$, $L(4, -4)$ and $J'(-9, 0)$, $K'(-3, 2)$, $L'(-12, -4)$

   b. $P(8, 6)$, $Q(-4, 12)$, $R(7, 7)$ and $P'(8, -20)$, $Q'(-4, -26)$, $R'(7, -21)$

10. Squash is a racket sport like tennis, except that the ball must bounce off a wall between returns. At what point on the front wall should player 1 aim at in order to reach the rear wall as far from player 2 as possible?

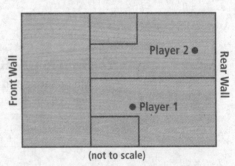

(not to scale)

EXPLORE & REASON

Draw a copy of *ABCD* on a grid. Using another color, draw a copy of *ABCD* on the grid in a different location with the same orientation, and label it *QRST*.

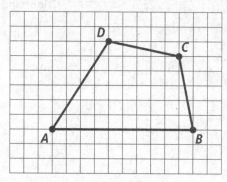

A. On another sheet of paper, write instructions that describe how to move *ABCD* to the location of *QRST*.

B. Exchange instructions with a partner. Follow your partner's instructions to draw a third shape *EFGH* in another color on the same grid. Compare your drawings. Do your drawings look the same? Explain.

C. Communicate Precisely What makes a set of instructions for this Explore & Reason a good set of instructions? Ⓒ **MP.6**

HABITS OF MIND

Use Appropriate Tools Why is placing the figures on a grid helpful in writing a set of instructions? Ⓒ **MP.5**

EXAMPLE 1

Try It! Find the Image of a Translation

1. What are the vertices of △E'F'G' produced by each translation?

   a. $T_{\langle 6, -7 \rangle}(\triangle EFG) = \triangle E'F'G'$

   b. △EFG is translated 11 units right and 2 units up

EXAMPLE 2

Try It! Write a Translation Rule

2. What translation rule maps $P(-3, 1)$ to its image $P'(2, 3)$?

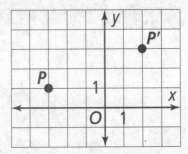

HABITS OF MIND

Communicate Precisely For Try Its 1 and 2, how might you explain what it means to move the same distance and in the same direction? ⓒ MP.6

EXAMPLE 3

Try It! Compose Translations

3. What is the composition of the transformations written as one transformation?

a. a translation 1 unit right and 1 unit down, then a translation 3 units right and 2 units down

b. $T_{\langle -4, 0\rangle} \circ T_{\langle -2, 5\rangle}$

HABITS OF MIND

Use Structure What do you notice about the order of composing two translations? © MP.7

EXAMPLE 4

Try It! Relate Translations and Reflections

4. Suppose n is the line with equation $y = 1$. Given $\triangle DEF$ with vertices $D(0, 0)$, $E(0, 3)$, and $F(3, 0)$, what translation image is equivalent to $(r_n \circ r_{x\text{-axis}})(\triangle DEF)$?

EXAMPLE 5

Try It! Prove Theorem 3-1

5. Theorem 3-1 states that a translation is a composition of reflections across two parallel lines. In the proof, given a translation T where $T(C) = C''$, let C' be the midpoint of $\overline{CC''}$, with $CC' = C'C'' = d$. For perpendicular bisectors m and n of $\overline{CC'}$ and $\overline{C'C''}$, you can show that $(r_n \circ r_m)(C) = C''$, where $CC'' = 2d$.

For a point B between m and n, as shown, show that $(r_n \circ r_m)(B) = T(B)$ where $BB'' = 2d$. To prove for any point B that $(r_n \circ r_m)(B) = T(B)$ where $BB'' = 2d$, what are the possible cases for the position of B relative to m and n that you need to consider?

HABITS OF MIND

Make Sense and Persevere When you want to choose two reflections to make a translation, what do you notice about the first line of reflection you choose? © MP.1

Do You UNDERSTAND?

1. **ESSENTIAL QUESTION** What are the properties of a translation?

2. **Error Analysis** Nori says that for any $\triangle XYZ$, the reflection over the y-axis composed with the reflection over the x-axis is equivalent to a translation of $\triangle XYZ$. Explain Nori's error.
© **MP.3**

3. **Vocabulary** Write an example of a composition of rigid motions for $\triangle PQR$.

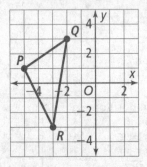

4. **Make Sense and Persevere** What are the values of x and y if $T_{\langle -2,\, 7\rangle}(x,\, y) = (3,\, -1)$?
© **MP.1**

Do You KNOW HOW?

For Exercises 5 and 6, the vertices of $\triangle XYZ$ are $X(1, -4)$, $Y(-2, -1)$, and $Z(3, 1)$. For each translation, give the vertices of $\triangle X'Y'Z'$.

5. $T_{\langle -4,\, -2\rangle}\,(\triangle XYZ)$ 6. $T_{\langle 5,\, -3\rangle}\,(\triangle XYZ)$

7. What is the rule for the translation shown?

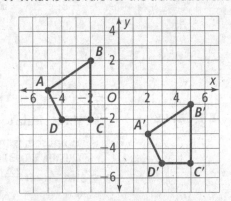

For Exercises 8 and 9, write the composition of translations as one translation.

8. $T_{\langle 7,\, 8\rangle} \circ T_{\langle -3,\, -4\rangle}$ 9. $T_{\langle 0,\, 3\rangle} \circ T_{\langle 4,\, 6\rangle}$

10. How far apart are two parallel lines m and n such that $T_{\langle 12,\, 0\rangle}(\triangle JKL) = (r_n \circ r_m)(\triangle JKL)$?

CRITIQUE & EXPLAIN

Filipe says that the next time one of the hands of the clock points to 7 will be at 7:00 when the hour hand points to 7. Nadia says that it will be at 5:35 when the minute hand points to 7.

A. Whose statement is correct? Explain.

B. **Communicate Precisely** Suppose the numbers on the clock face are removed. Write instructions that another person could follow to move the minute hand from 2 to 6. Ⓒ **MP.6**

HABITS OF MIND

Generalize How are rotating and translating a figure alike? How are they different? Ⓒ **MP.8**

EXAMPLE 1

Try It! Draw a Rotated Image

1. Do you think a rotated image would ever coincide with the original figure? Explain.

EXAMPLE 2

Try It! Draw Rotations in the Coordinate Plane

2. The vertices of $\triangle XYZ$ are $X(-4, 7)$, $Y(0, 8)$, and $Z(2, -1)$.

   a. What are the vertices of $R_{(180°,\, O)}(\triangle XYZ)$?

   b. What are the vertices of $R_{(270°,\, O)}(\triangle XYZ)$?

EXAMPLE 3

Try It! Use Rotations

3. a. The illustration shows a drumline transformed by the rotation $R_{(180°,\, A)}$ and then by $R_{(-135°,\, B')}$. Suppose the drumline instead turns counterclockwise about B' for the second rotation. How many degrees must it rotate so that the drummer originally at A ends up at A'' as before?

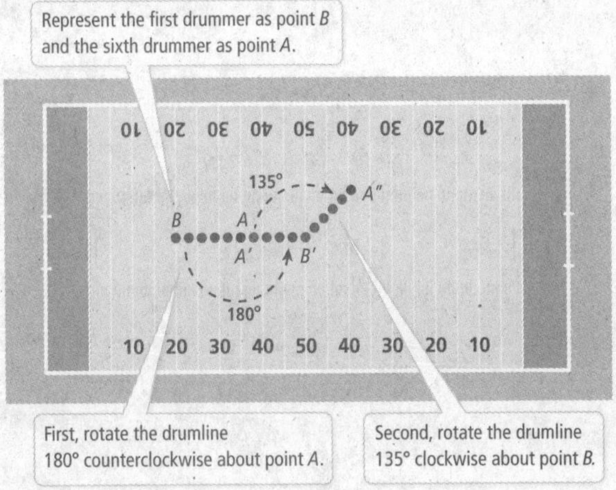

   Represent the first drummer as point B and the sixth drummer as point A.

   b. Can the composition of rotations be described by $R_{(45°,\, A)}$ since $180° - 135° = 45°$? Explain.

   First, rotate the drumline 180° counterclockwise about point A.

   Second, rotate the drumline 135° clockwise about point B.

HABITS OF MIND

Make Sense and Persevere What information do you need in order to find the image of one or more rotations? ⓒ MP.1

EXAMPLE 4

Try It! Investigate Reflections and Rotations

4. The diagram shows *JKLM* and its image *WXYZ* after being rotated about point *T*. You can obtain the same result using two reflections. First, draw a line *p* through *T*, and reflect *JKLM* across *p* to form *J'K'L'M'*. The midpoints of the segments connecting corresponding points of *J'K'L'M'* and *WXYZ* are collinear with *T*. Reflecting *J'K'L'M'* across this line gives *WXYZ*.

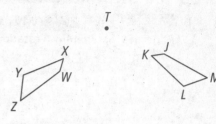

Follow the same constructions, but instead draw line *p* so that it does not pass through *T*. Do you get the same results? Explain.

EXAMPLE 5

Try It! Prove Theorem 3-2

5. Theorem 3-2 states that any rotation is a composition of reflections across two lines that intersect at the center of rotation, and the angle of rotation is twice the angle formed by the lines of reflection. In the figure, $R_{(X°, P)}(A) = B$. Point *A* is reflected across a line *m* passing through a point *Q* not on *PA*. Point *A*'s image *A'* is then reflected across line *n*, which bisects ∠*BPA'*, resulting in *A″* = *B*. The conclusion about the angles follows quickly.

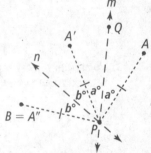

Suppose point *Q* is closer to point *B* or even outside of ∠*APB*. Does the relationship still hold for the angle between the reflection lines and the angle between the preimage and the image? Explain.

HABITS OF MIND

Use Structure How can you tell if two lines of reflection will result in a rotation? ⓒ MP.7

Do You UNDERSTAND?

1. **ESSENTIAL QUESTION** What are the properties that identify a rotation?

2. **Error Analysis** Isabel drew the diagram below to show the rotation of △DEF about point T. What is her error? © MP.3

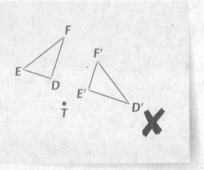

3. **Vocabulary** How is the *center of rotation* related to the *center of a circle*?

4. **Construct Arguments** In the diagram, △A″B″C″ is the image of reflections of △ABC across lines p and q. It is also the image of a rotation of △ABC about R. What is the angle of rotation? Explain. © MP.3

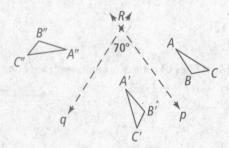

Do You KNOW HOW?

Trace each figure and draw its rotated image.

5. $R_{(90°,\ P)}(\overline{MN})$

6. $R_{(120°,\ T)}(\triangle ABC)$

Give the coordinates of each image.

7. $R_{(180°,\ O)}(\overline{GH})$ for G(2, −9), H(−1, 3)

8. a rotation of △XYZ 90° about the origin for X(0, 3), Y(1, −4), Z(5, 2)

Construct two lines of reflection such that the composition of the reflections across the lines maps onto the image shown.

9.

10.

CRITIQUE & EXPLAIN

Two students are trying to determine whether compositions of rigid motions are commutative. Paula translates a triangle and then reflects it across a line. When she reflects and then translates, she gets the same image. She concludes that compositions of rigid motions are commutative.

Translate. Then reflect.

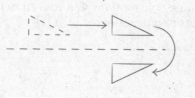

Reflect. Then translate.

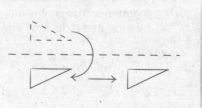

Keenan rotates a triangle and then reflects it. When he changes the order of the rigid motions, he gets a different image. He concludes that compositions of rigid motions are not commutative.

Rotate. Then reflect.

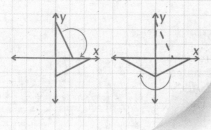

Reflect. Then rotate.

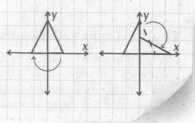

A. Should Paula have used grid paper? Explain.

B. Communicate Precisely Do you agree with Paula or with Keenan? Explain. © MP.6

HABITS OF MIND

Communicate Precisely What should you look for to determine whether two given rigid motions are commutative? © MP.6

EXAMPLE 1

Try It! Prove Theorem 3-3

1. Theorem 3-3 states that the composition of two or more rigid motions is a rigid motion. For two rigid motions T and S, this means that $S \circ T$ is a rigid motion. For three noncollinear points P, Q, and R where $P'Q'R'$ is the image of PQR after T and $P''Q''R''$ is the image of $P'Q'R'$ after S, you can use the Transitive Property of Equality to show that length and angle measure are preserved: $PQ = P''Q''$ and $m\angle PQR = m\angle P''Q''R''$.

Describe how you can use the same reasoning to show that the theorem is true when composing three rigid motions. Can your strategy be extended to include any number of rigid motions?

EXAMPLE 2

Try It! Explore Glide Reflections

2. The grid shows $\triangle ABC$ reflected across the line with equation $x = -1$, then translated 5 units down. Draw the image of $\triangle ABC$ translated 5 units down, then reflected across the line with equation $x = -1$. What conclusion can you draw about the order of the rigid motions in a glide reflection?

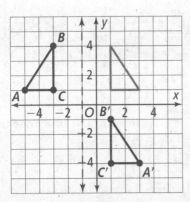

HABITS OF MIND

Use Structure What observations do you make about a figure to determine the type of rigid motion? Ⓒ MP.7

EXAMPLE 3

Try It! Find the Image of a Glide Reflection

3. Quadrilateral *RSTV* has vertices *R*(−3, 2), *S*(0, 5), *T*(4, −4), and *V*(0, −2). Use the rule $T_{\langle 1, 0 \rangle} \circ r_{x\text{-axis}}$ to graph and label the glide reflection of *RSTV*.

EXAMPLE 4

Try It! Determine a Glide Reflection

4. What is the glide reflection that maps each of the following?

   a. △*ABC* → △*A′B′C′* given *A*(−3, 4), *B*(−4, 2), *C*(−1, 1), *A′*(1, 1), *B′*(2, −1), and *C′*(−1, −2).

   b. $\overline{RS} \to \overline{R'S'}$ given *R*(−2, 4), *S*(2, 6), *R′*(4, 0), and *S′*(8, −2).

HABITS OF MIND

Make Sense and Persevere What other strategy could you use to find a glide reflection? ⓒ MP.1

Do You UNDERSTAND?

1. **ESSENTIAL QUESTION** How are properties of the four types of rigid motions similar or different?

2. Is it correct to say that the composition of a translation followed by a reflection is a glide reflection? Explain.

3. **Error Analysis** Tamika draws the following diagram as an example of a glide reflection. What error did she make? © MP.3

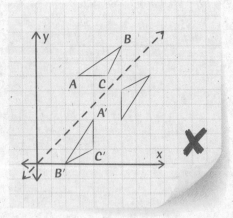

Do You KNOW HOW?

Use the figures for Exercises 4–7. Identify each rigid motion as a translation, a reflection, a rotation, or a glide reflection.

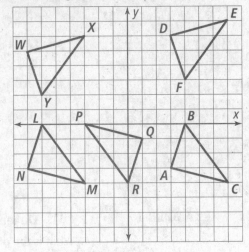

4. △WYX → △NLM

5. △DFE → △WYX

6. △WYX → △ABC

7. △NLM → △QRP

EXPLORE & REASON

Look at the kaleidoscope image shown. Then consider pieces A and B taken from the image.

Piece A   Piece B

A. How are piece A and piece B related? Describe a rigid motion that you can use on piece B to produce piece A.

B. Communicate Precisely Describe a composition of rigid motions that you can use on piece A to produce the image. ⓒ **MP.6**

C. How many rigid motions did you need to produce the image from piece A? Can you think of another composition of rigid motions to produce the image starting with piece A?

HABITS OF MIND

Reason What part of the figure is piece A? How does that fraction relate to the number of rigid motions needed to produce the entire figure? ⓒ **MP.2**

EXAMPLE 1

Try It! Identify Transformations for Symmetry

1. What transformations map each figure onto itself?

a.

b.

EXAMPLE 2

Try It! Identify Lines of Symmetry

2. How many lines of symmetry does each figure have? How do you know whether you have found them all?

a.

b.

EXAMPLE 3

Try It! Identify Rotational Symmetry

3. What are the rotational symmetries for each figure? Does each figure have point symmetry?

a.

b.
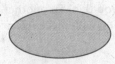

c.

d.

··

HABITS OF MIND

Use Structure How do you know if you have found all lines of symmetry to a figure? ⓒ MP.7

EXAMPLE 4

Try It! Determine Symmetries

4. What symmetries does a square have?

EXAMPLE 5

Try It! Use Symmetry

5. What is a possible design for a circular logo that looks the same for each 60° rotation and uses at least two colors?

HABITS OF MIND

Make Sense and Persevere What steps can you take to determine if a figure has symmetry? ⓒ **MP.1**

Do You UNDERSTAND?

1. **ESSENTIAL QUESTION** How can you tell whether a figure is symmetric?

2. **Error Analysis** For the figure below, Adam was asked to draw all lines of reflection. His work is shown. What error did Adam make? ⒸMP.3

3. **Vocabulary** What type of symmetry does a figure have if it can be mapped onto itself by being flipped over a line?

4. **Communicate Precisely** What does it mean for a figure to have 60° rotational symmetry? ⒸMP.6

5. **Construct Arguments** Is it possible for a figure to have rotational symmetry and no reflectional symmetry? Explain or give examples. ⒸMP.3

Do You KNOW HOW?

Find the number of lines of symmetry for each figure.

6.

7.

Describe the rotational symmetry of each figure. State whether each has point symmetry.

8.

9.

Identify the types of symmetry of each figure. For each figure with reflectional symmetry, identify the lines of symmetry. For each figure with rotational symmetry, identify the angles of rotation that map the figure onto itself.

10.

11.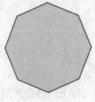

The Perplexing Polygon

Look around and you will see shapes and patterns everywhere you look. The tiles on a floor are often all the same shape and fit together to form a pattern. The petals on a flower often make a repeating pattern around the center of the flower. When you look at snowflakes under a microscope, you'll notice that they are made up of repeating three-dimensional crystals. Think about this during the Mathematical Modeling in 3 Acts lesson.

ACT 1 ▸ Identify the Problem

1. What is the first question that comes to mind after watching the video?

2. Write down the main question you will answer.

3. Make an initial conjecture that answers this main question.

4. Explain how you arrived at your conjecture.

5. What information will be useful to know to answer the main question? How can you get it? How will you use that information?

ACT 2 ▶ Develop a Model

6. Use the math that you have learned in this Topic to refine your conjecture.

ACT 3 ▶ Interpret the Results

7. Did your refined conjecture match the actual answer exactly? If not, what might explain the difference?

EXPLORE & REASON

Some corporate logos are distinctive because they make use of repeated shapes. Below are some logo mockups for a renewable energy company.

A designer creates two versions of a new logo for the company. Version 1 uses the original image shown at the right and a reflection of it. Version 2 uses reduced copies of the original image.

A. Make a sketch of each version.

B. Communicate Precisely The owner of the company says, "I like your designs, but it is important that the transformed image be the same size and shape as the original image." What would you do to comply with the owner's requirements? © **MP.6**

C. What transformations can you apply to the original image that would produce logos acceptable to the owner? Explain.

HABITS OF MIND

Use Structure Is comparing the measures of all the angles in a preimage and in an image sufficient to guarantee the figures are congruent? © **MP.7**

EXAMPLE 1

Try It! Understand Congruence

1. A 90° rotation about the origin maps △PQR to △LMN. Are the triangles congruent? Explain.

EXAMPLE 2

Try It! Verify Congruence

2. Use the graph shown.

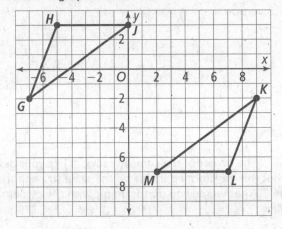

a. Given △GHJ ≅ △KLM, what is one composition of rigid motions that maps △GHJ to △KLM?

b. What is another composition of rigid motions that maps △GHJ to △KLM?

- -

HABITS OF MIND

Construct Arguments Can a figure be congruent to itself? ⓒ MP.3

EXAMPLE 3

Try It! Identify Congruent Figures

3. Use the graph shown.

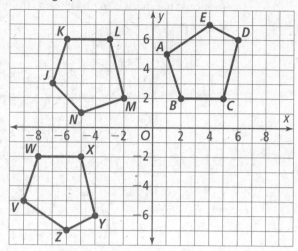

a. Are *ABCDE* and *JKLMN* congruent? If so, describe a composition of rigid motions that maps *ABCDE* to *JKLMN*. If not, explain.

b. Are *ABCDE* and *VWXYZ* congruent? If so, describe a composition of rigid motions that maps *ABCDE* to *VWXYZ*. If not, explain.

EXAMPLE 4

Try It! Determine Congruence

4. Is the pair of objects congruent? If so, describe a composition of rigid motions that maps one object onto the other.

a.

b.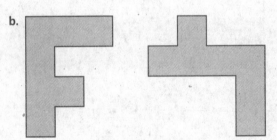

HABITS OF MIND

Use Structure If one part of an image is congruent to the corresponding part of the preimage, does that mean the entire image and preimage must be congruent? © MP.7

EXAMPLE 5

Try It! Apply Congruence

5. Unit A can be mapped to Unit B with a rotation 180°
   about its top left corner, then a translation right and
   down. What is another composition of rigid motions
   that shows Unit A is congruent to Unit B?

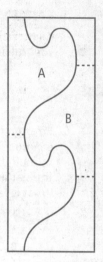

HABITS OF MIND

Model With Mathematics How can you determine whether two real-world
figures are congruent? ⓒ MP.4

Do You UNDERSTAND?

1. **ESSENTIAL QUESTION** What is the relationship between rigid motions and congruence?

2. **Error Analysis** Taylor says *ABCD* and *EFGH* are congruent because he can map *ABCD* to *EFGH* by multiplying each side length by 1.5 and translating the result to coincide with *EFGH*. What is Taylor's error? © MP.3

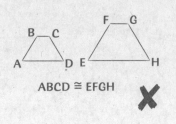

ABCD ≅ EFGH

3. **Vocabulary** Why is a rigid motion also called a congruence transformation?

4. **Reason** For any two line segments that are congruent, what must be true about the lengths of the segments? © MP.2

5. **Construct Arguments** A composition of rigid motions maps one figure to another figure. Is each intermediate image in the composition congruent to the original and final figures? Explain. © MP.3

6. **Communicate Precisely** Describe how you can find a rigid motion or composition of rigid motions to map a segment to a congruent segment and an angle to a congruent angle. © MP.6

Do You KNOW HOW?

7. Given *ABCD* ≅ *EFGH*, what rigid motion, or composition of rigid motions, maps *ABCD* to *EFGH*?

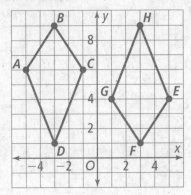

8. Which triangles are congruent?

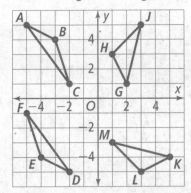

9. Are Figure A and Figure B congruent? If so, describe a composition of rigid motions that maps Figure A to Figure B. If not, explain.

Figure A   Figure B

EXPLORE & REASON

Cut out a triangle with two sides of equal length from a sheet of paper and label its angles 1, 2, and 3. Trace the outline of your triangle on another sheet of paper and label the angles.

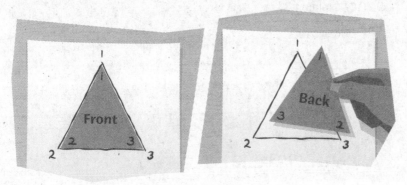

A. In how many different ways can you flip, slide, or turn the triangle so that it fits exactly on the outline?

B. Look for Relationships How do the angles and sides of the outline correspond to the angles and sides of the triangle? © MP.7

C. How would your answer to Part A change if all three sides of the triangle were of equal length?

HABITS OF MIND

Generalize Will this process work with any other triangles? Explain. © MP.8

EXAMPLE 1

Try It! Understand Angles of Isosceles Triangles

1. Reflect △ABC across line BC to create the image △A'B'C'. What is another rigid motion that maps △A'B'C' onto △ABC? Can you use this to show that ∠A ≅ ∠C? Explain.

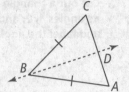

EXAMPLE 2

Try It! Use the Isosceles Triangle Theorem

2. What is the value of x?

a.

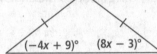

   (5x + 9)°
   28°

b.

   (−4x + 9)°   (8x − 3)°

HABITS OF MIND

Communicate Precisely Given the angle measure of the vertex angle, how can you find the measures of the base angles? © MP.6

EXAMPLE 3

Try It! Use the Converse of the Isosceles Triangle Theorem

3. Use the figure shown.

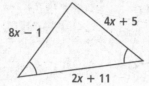

8x − 1   4x + 5

2x + 11

a. What is the value of x?

b. What are the lengths of all three sides of the triangle?

EXAMPLE 4

Try It! Use Perpendicular Bisectors to Solve Problems

4. Use the figure shown.

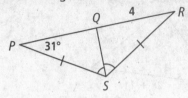

a. What is $m\angle RSQ$?

b. What is PR?

HABITS OF MIND

Generalize How do you know that any isosceles triangle can be decomposed into two congruent right triangles? © MP.8

EXAMPLE 5

Try It! Prove that Equilateral Triangles are Equiangular

5. What rotation can be used to show the angles of an equilateral triangle are congruent?

EXAMPLE 6

Try It! Use Angles in Isosceles and Equilateral Triangles

6. Find each angle measure in the figure.

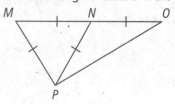

a. $m\angle PNO$

b. $m\angle NOP$

HABITS OF MIND

Reason How do you know what the measures of the angles of an equilateral triangle are? Ⓒ MP.2

Do You UNDERSTAND?

1. **ESSENTIAL QUESTION** How are the side lengths and angle measures related in isosceles triangles and in equilateral triangles?

2. **Error Analysis** Nate drew the following diagram to represent an isosceles triangle sharing a side with an equilateral triangle. What mistake did Nate make? © MP.3

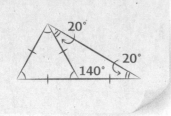

3. **Vocabulary** What is the difference between the base and a leg of an isosceles triangle?

4. **Reason** Is it possible for the vertex of an isosceles triangle to be a right angle? Explain why or why not, and state the angle measures of the triangle, if possible. © MP.2

5. **Communicate Precisely** Describe five rigid motions that map equilateral triangle △PQR onto itself. © MP.6

Do You KNOW HOW?

For Exercises 6 and 7, find the unknown angle measures.

6.

7.

For Exercises 8 and 9, find the lengths of all three sides of the triangle.

8.

9.
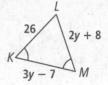

10. What is $m\angle ABD$ in the figure shown?

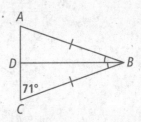

11. A light is attached to a cable and suspended between two poles that are each 9.5 feet tall. How far above the ground is the light? Round to the nearest tenth of a foot.

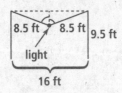

Check It Out!

Maybe you've played this game before: you draw a picture. Then you try to get a classmate to draw the same picture by giving step-by-step directions but without showing your drawings.

Try it with a classmate. Draw a map of a room in your house or a place in your town. Then give directions to a classmate to draw the map that you drew. How similar are they? Think about this during the Mathematical Modeling in 3 Acts lesson.

MATHEMATICAL MODELING IN **3** ACTS

SavvasRealize.com

ACT 1 **Identify the Problem**

1. What is the first question that comes to mind after watching the video?

2. Write down the main question you will answer about what you saw in the video.

3. Make an initial conjecture that answers this main question.

4. Explain how you arrived at your conjecture.

5. What information will be useful to know to answer the main question? How can you get it? How will you use that information?

ACT 2 — Develop a Model

6. Use the math that you have learned in this Topic to refine your conjecture.

ACT 3 — Interpret the Results

7. Did your refined conjecture match the actual answer exactly? If not, what might explain the difference?

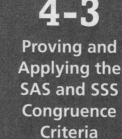
EXPLORE & REASON

Make five triangles that have a 5-inch side, a 6-inch side, and one 40° angle.

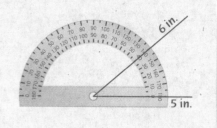

A. How many unique triangles can you make?

B. Construct Arguments How are the unique triangles different from each other? © MP.3

HABITS OF MIND

Make Sense and Persevere How could you organize your work to make sure you have tried every possible combination of the given side lengths and angle measure? © MP.1

EXAMPLE 1

Try It! Explore the Side-Angle-Side (SAS) Congruence Criterion

1. What rigid motion or composition of rigid motions shows that △*UVW* maps to △*XYZ*?

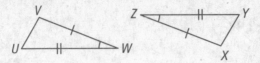

EXAMPLE 2

Try It! Apply the SAS Congruence Criterion

2. Given that $\overline{AB} \parallel \overline{CD}$ and $\overline{AB} \cong \overline{CD}$, how can you show that ∠*B* ≅ ∠*D*?

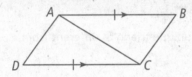

- -

HABITS OF MIND

Reason How can knowing lines are parallel help establish triangle congruence by SAS? ⓒ MP.2

EXAMPLE 3

Try It! Prove the Side-Side-Side (SSS) Congruence Criterion

3. What composition of rigid motions maps △PQR to △STU?

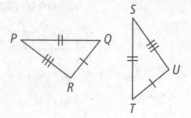

EXAMPLE 4

Try It! Determine Congruent Triangles

4. Determine if the triangles are congruent. If it cannot be determined, what additional information is needed to show the triangles are congruent?

a.

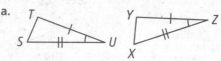

b.

HABITS OF MIND

Look for Relationships How can you decide whether to choose either SAS or SSS to prove triangle congruence? Ⓒ MP.7

Do You UNDERSTAND?

1. ESSENTIAL QUESTION How are SAS and SSS used to show that two triangles are congruent?

2. Error Analysis Elijah says △ABC and △DEF are congruent by SAS. Explain Elijah's error. © MP.3

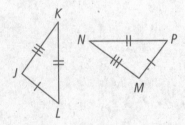

3. Construct Arguments Suppose $\overline{PR} \cong \overline{ST}$ and ∠P ≅ ∠S. Ron wants prove △PQR ≅ △STU by SAS. He says that all he needs to do is to show $\overline{RQ} \cong \overline{SU}$. Will that work? Explain. © MP.3

4. Reason How would you decide what theorem to use to prove ∠JKL ≅ ∠MNP? Explain. © MP.2

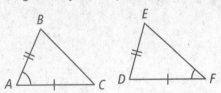

5. Make Sense and Persevere Suppose that $\overline{JK}$ and $\overline{LM}$ bisect each other. Is there enough information to show that △JPM ≅ △KPL? Explain. © MP.1

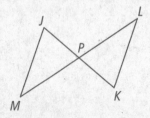

Do You KNOW HOW?

For Exercises 6–8, which pairs of triangles are congruent by SAS? By SSS?

6.

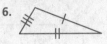

7.

8.

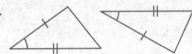

For Exercises 9–11, are the triangles congruent? Explain.

9.

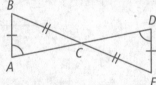

10.

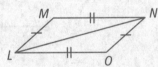

11.

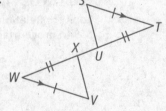

EXPLORE & REASON

Are these triangles congruent?

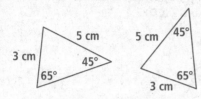

A. Make Sense and Persevere Assume the triangles are *not* congruent. What contradictions can you find to contradict your assumption? Explain. ⓒ **MP.1**

B. Is it sufficient to say that the triangles are congruent because of the contradictions you found? Explain.

HABITS OF MIND

Generalize Is there a mathematical rule for proving that these triangles are congruent? ⓒ **MP.8**

EXAMPLE 1

Try It! Explore the Angle-Side-Angle (ASA) Congruence Criterion

1. What is the relationship between *BX* and *CY*? What conclusion can you draw about the relationship of △*AXB* and △*CDY*?

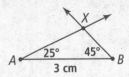 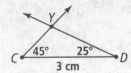

EXAMPLE 2

Try It! Prove the Angle-Side-Angle (ASA) Congruence Criterion

2. Describe a series of transformations that shows △*JKL* ≅ △*MNO*.

EXAMPLE 3

Try It! **Apply the Angle-Side-Angle (ASA) Congruence Criterion**

3. Use the figures shown.

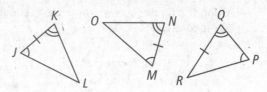

a. Are △JKL and △MNO congruent? Explain.

b. Are △JKL and △PQR congruent? Explain.

HABITS OF MIND

Communicate Precisely What properties can you use to show that angles are congruent? ⓒ MP.6

EXAMPLE 4

Try It! Investigate the Angle-Angle-Side (AAS) Congruence Criterion

4. Using the figures shown, describe a sequence of rigid motions that maps △JKL to △QRP.

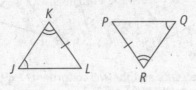

EXAMPLE 5

Try It! Use Triangle Congruence Criteria

5. Use the figures shown.

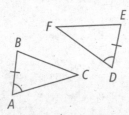

a. What additional information is needed to show △ABC ≅ △DEF by ASA?

b. What additional information is needed to show △ABC ≅ △DEF by AAS?

- -

HABITS OF MIND

Construct Arguments How can it be helpful to assume the opposite of what you have been asked to prove? © MP.3

EXAMPLE 6

Try It! Determine Congruent Polygons

6. Given $ABCD \cong EFGH$, what is the value of x?

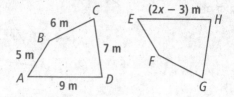

HABITS OF MIND

Generalize How does identifying congruent triangles help you show that polygons are congruent? Ⓒ MP.8

Do You UNDERSTAND?

1. **ESSENTIAL QUESTION** How are ASA and AAS used to show that triangles are congruent?

2. **Error Analysis** Why is Terrell's conclusion incorrect? © MP.3

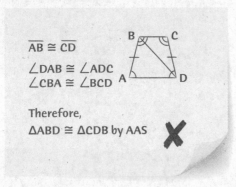

$\overline{AB} \cong \overline{CD}$

$\angle DAB \cong \angle ADC$
$\angle CBA \cong \angle BCD$

Therefore,
$\triangle ABD \cong \triangle CDB$ by AAS ✗

3. **Reason** How can you tell which property of triangle congruence shows $\triangle RST \cong \triangle UVW$? © MP.2

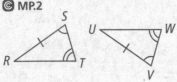

4. **Make Sense and Persevere** Is there a congruence relationship that is sufficient to show that $\triangle MNO \cong \triangle TUV$? Explain. © MP.1

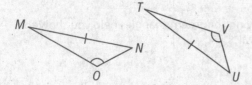

Do You KNOW HOW?

For Exercises 5 and 6, find the value of x.

5.

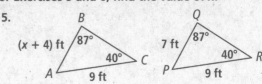

6.

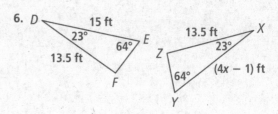

For Exercises 7 and 8, state whether the triangles are congruent and by which theorem.

7.

8.

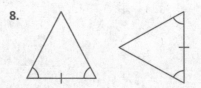

9. Why is $LMNO \cong PQRS$?

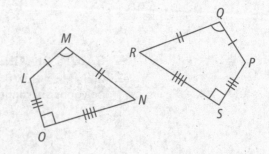

CRITIQUE & EXPLAIN

Seth and Jae wrote the following explanations of why the two triangles are congruent.

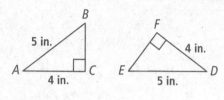

Seth

Jae

There are two pairs of congruent sides, $\overline{AB} \cong \overline{DE}$ and $\overline{AC} \cong \overline{DF}$, and a pair of congruent right angles, $\angle C \cong \angle F$. So $\triangle ABC \cong \triangle DEF$ by SSA.

The lengths of $\overline{BC}$ and $\overline{EF}$ are 3 in., since these are 3-4-5 right triangles. There are three pairs of congruent sides, $\overline{AB} \cong \overline{DE}$, $\overline{AC} \cong \overline{DF}$, and $\overline{BC} \cong \overline{EF}$. So $\triangle ABC \cong \triangle DEF$ by SSS.

A. Do you think either student is correct? Explain.

B. Communicate Precisely Describe when you can state that two right triangles are congruent if you are only given two pairs of congruent sides and a right angle in each triangle. Ⓒ MP.6

HABITS OF MIND

Make Sense and Persevere Could you use Jae's strategy if the dimensions of the triangles were different? Ⓒ MP.1

EXAMPLE 1

Try It! Investigate Right Triangle Congruence

1. Can you show that two right triangles are congruent when any one pair of corresponding acute angles is congruent and any one pair of corresponding legs is congruent? Explain.

EXAMPLE 2

Try It! Use the Hypotenuse-Leg (HL) Theorem

2. What information is needed in order to apply the Hypotenuse-Leg (HL) Theorem?

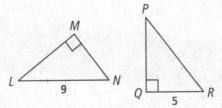

HABITS OF MIND

Look for Relationships What are the relationships that you could use to show that two right triangles are congruent? Ⓒ MP.7

EXAMPLE 3

Try It! Write a Proof Using the Hypotenuse-Leg (HL) Theorem

3. Write a proof to show that two triangles are congruent.

Given: $\overline{JL} \perp \overline{KM}$, $\overline{JK} \cong \overline{LK}$

Prove: $\triangle JKM \cong \triangle LKM$

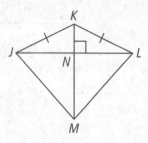

HABITS OF MIND

Make Sense and Persevere What observations do you need to make to write a proof showing that two triangles are congruent? Ⓒ MP.1

Do You UNDERSTAND?

1. **ESSENTIAL QUESTION** What minimum criteria are needed to show that right triangles are congruent?

2. **Error Analysis** Yama stated that △KLM ≅ △PLN by the HL Theorem. What mistake did Yama make? © MP.3

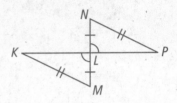

3. **Use Structure** What are the three conditions that two triangles must meet in order to apply the HL Theorem? © MP.7

4. **Reason** The HL Theorem is a side-side-angle theorem for right triangles. Why does it prove congruence for two right triangles but not prove congruence for two acute triangles or for two obtuse triangles? © MP.2

Do You KNOW HOW?

What information is needed to prove the triangles are congruent using the Hypotenuse-Leg (HL) Theorem?

5.

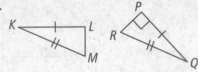

6.

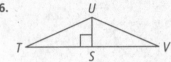

What information would be sufficient to show the two triangles are congruent by the Hypotenuse-Leg (HL) Theorem?

7.

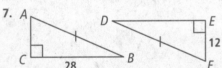

8.

EXPLORE & REASON

Look at the painting shown.

A. How many triangles can you find?

B. Make Sense and Persevere What strategy did you use to count the triangles? How well did your strategy work? © **MP.1**

HABITS OF MIND

Make Sense and Persevere What are some other strategies you might try to help you find all the triangles? © **MP.1**

EXAMPLE 1

Try It! Identify Corresponding Parts in Triangles

1. What are the corresponding sides and angles in △FHJ and △KHG?

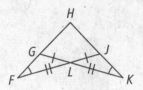

EXAMPLE 2

Try It! Use Common Parts of Triangles

2. Are $\overline{VW}$ and $\overline{ZY}$ congruent? Explain.

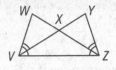

HABITS OF MIND

Generalize Could there be more than one correct way to assign corresponding vertices in two congruent triangles? Explain. © MP.8

EXAMPLE 3

Try It! Prove That Two Triangles Are Congruent

3. Write a proof to show that △SRV ≅ △TUW.

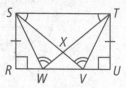

EXAMPLE 4

Try It! Separate Overlapping Triangles

4. A new bus route for the area of a city shown will stop at the History Museum, Water Park, Zoo, Science Museum, and Theater. Draw a triangle to represent the new route. Include any length or angle information that is given in the diagram.

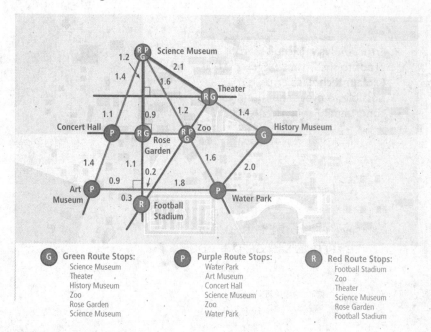

HABITS OF MIND

Look for Relationships What observations do you make about the different ways triangles can overlap? ⒸMP.7

Do You UNDERSTAND?

1. **ESSENTIAL QUESTION** Which theorems can be used to prove two overlapping triangles are congruent?

2. **Construct Arguments** How could you prove that △ACD ≅ △ECB? © MP.3

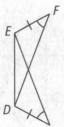

3. **Error Analysis** Nicholas wrote a proof to show that △EFD ≅ △DGE. Explain Nicholas's error. Is it possible to prove the triangles congruent? Explain. © MP.3

Since $\overline{EF} \cong \overline{DG}$, $\angle F \cong \angle G$, and $\overline{ED} \cong \overline{ED}$, by SAS, △EFD ≅ △DGE. ✗

4. **Use Structure** Quadrilateral JKLM is a rectangle. Which triangles are congruent to △JKL? Explain. © MP.7

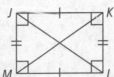

Do You KNOW HOW?

5. What are the corresponding sides and angles in △WXV and △XWY?

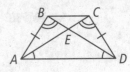

In Exercises 6–9, name a side or angle congruent to each given side or angle.

6. ∠CDA

7. $\overline{DB}$

8. ∠FGH

9. $\overline{HJ}$

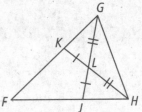

For Exercises 10 and 11, name a theorem that can be used to prove that each pair of triangles is congruent.

10. △GJL and △KHL   11. △NQM and △PMQ

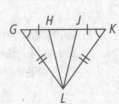 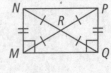

MODEL AND DISCUSS

A new high school will be built for **Brighton** and **Springfield**. The location of the school must be the same distance from each middle school. The distance between the two middle schools is 18 miles.

Brighton Middle School

Springfield Middle School

A. Trace the points for the schools on a piece of paper. Locate a new point that is 12 mi from each school. Compare your point with the points of other students. Is there more than one location for the new high school? Explain.

B. Reason Can you find locations for the new high school that are the same distance from each middle school for any given distance? Explain. ⓒ MP.2

HABITS OF MIND

Reason Are there any potential locations that are less than 9 miles from each middle school? Explain. ⓒ MP.2

EXAMPLE 1

Try It! Find Equidistant Points

1. Draw a pair of fixed points, and find points that are equidistant from the two fixed points. Draw a line through the set of equidistant points. Repeat this process for several pairs of fixed points. What conjecture can you make about points that are the same distance from a given pair of points?

EXAMPLE 2

Try It! Prove the Perpendicular Bisector Theorem

2. Prove the Converse of the Perpendicular Bisector Theorem.

   If a point is equidistant from the endpoints of a segment, then it is on the perpendicular bisector of the segment.

If...

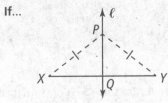

Then... $XQ = YQ$ and $\overleftrightarrow{PQ} \perp \overline{XY}$

- -

HABITS OF MIND

Construct Arguments You need to prove $PX = PY$. Which triangles have $\overline{PX}$ or $\overline{PY}$ as a side? © MP.3

EXAMPLE 3

Try It! Construct a Perpendicular Line

3. Construct the perpendicular bisector of $\overline{JK}$.

HABITS OF MIND

Reason Why are circles important in constructing points, segments, lines, and angles? ⓒ **MP.2**

EXAMPLE 4

Try It! Construct a Perpendicular Line

4. **a.** Construct a line perpendicular to line *m* through point *A*.

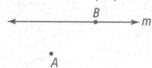

b. Construct a line perpendicular to line *m* through point *B*.

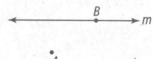

EXAMPLE 5

Try It! Use Constructions of Perpendicular Lines

5. Mr. Lee locates his ice cream cart at point *T*. Ms. Medina wants to position her souvenir cart on the other side of Main Street so that she is directly across from Mr. Lee's ice cream cart. How can Ms. Medina determine where to put her cart?

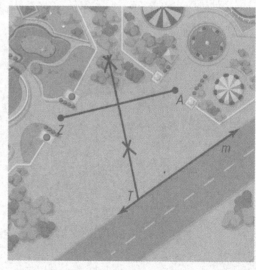

HABITS OF MIND

Look for Relationships Suppose the perpendicular bisector of $\overline{AZ}$ is $\overline{MT}$, and *M* is the midpoint of $\overline{AZ}$. What equation shows the relationship between *ZM*, *MT*, and *TZ*? Explain. ⓒ **MP.7**

EXAMPLE 6

Try It! Apply the Perpendicular Bisector Theorem

6. a. What is the value of *WY*?

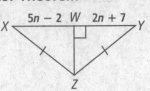

b. What is the value of *OL*?

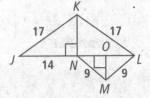

EXAMPLE 7

Try It! Find Equidistant Points from the Sides of an Angle

7. An airport baggage inspector stands equidistant from the two baggage conveyor belts. Consider two triangles that result from drawing perpendicular segments from where the inspector stands to the conveyor belts. How are the triangles related? Explain.

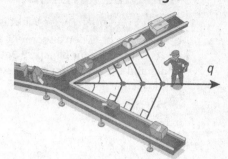

EXAMPLE 8

Try It! Apply the Angle Bisector Theorem

8. Use the figure shown.

   a. If $HI = 7$, $IJ = 7$, and $m\angle HGI = 25$, what is $m\angle IGJ$?

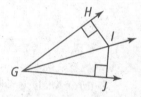

   b. If $m\angle HGJ = 57$, $m\angle IGJ = 28.5$, and $HI = 12.2$, what is the value of IJ?

- -

HABITS OF MIND

Communicate Precisely What do you need to know about a figure in order to use the Converse of the Angle Bisector Theorem? © MP.6

Do You UNDERSTAND?

1. **ESSENTIAL QUESTION** What is the relationship between a segment and the points on its perpendicular bisector? Between an angle and the points on its bisector?

2. **Vocabulary** How can you determine if a point is *equidistant* from the sides of an angle?

3. **Error Analysis** Dionne says that $\overrightarrow{KM}$ is the bisector of $\angle LKJ$ because $LM = MJ$. Explain the error in her reasoning. © MP.3

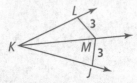

4. **Construct Arguments** You know that $\overline{AB}$ is the perpendicular bisector of $\overline{XY}$, and $\overline{XY}$ is the perpendicular bisector of $\overline{AB}$. What can you conclude about the side lengths of quadrilateral *AXBY*? Explain. © MP.3

Do You KNOW HOW?

5. If $JL = 14$, $KL = 10$, and $ML = 7$, what is JK?

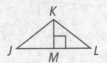

Use the figure shown for Exercises 6 and 7.

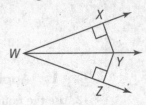

6. If $\angle XWY \cong \angle ZWY$ and $XY = 4$, what is YZ?

7. If $XY = ZY$ and $m\angle ZWY = 18$, what iºs $m\angle XWZ$?

8. What is an algebraic expression for the area of the square picture frame?

$x - 2$ in.

MODEL & DISCUSS

A town has three recycling sites. They want to build a parking garage for the recycling trucks so that the distances from the sites to the parking garage are as close to equal as possible.

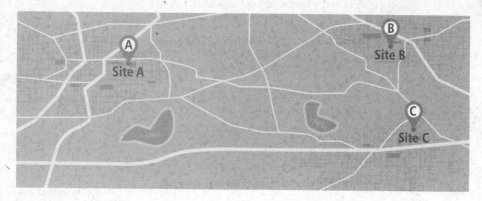

A. Points *A*, *B*, and *C* represent the locations of the three sites. Trace the points on a piece of paper. Locate a point *D* that appears to be the same distance from *A*, *B*, and *C* by sight only.

B. **Communicate Precisely** Measure the lengths from points *A*, *B*, and *C* to point *D* on your diagram. Are the lengths equal? If not, can you find a better location for point *D*? Explain. © MP.6

C. What do you think is the quickest way to find the best point *D* in similar situations?

HABITS OF MIND

Reason Suppose site *C* will be moved to a new location. Is it possible for *C* to move to a location where *D* will not be inside the triangle? Explain. © MP.2

EXAMPLE 1

Try It! Prove Theorem 5-5

1. Verify the Concurrency of Perpendicular Bisectors Theorem on acute, right, and obtuse triangles using a straightedge and compass or geometry software.

    Given: △ABC with perpendicular bisectors q, r, and s.

    Prove: Lines q, r, and s are concurrent at a point that is equidistant from A, B, and C.

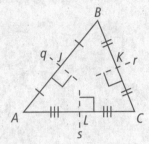

EXAMPLE 2

Try It! Investigate Circumscribed Circles

2. What conjecture can you make about the location of the circumcenter (the point of concurrency of the perpendicular bisectors of a triangle) for acute, right, and obtuse triangle?

HABITS OF MIND

Use Structure Consider the triangle in Example 1. Using vertices A, B, and C, midpoints J, K, and L, and circumcenter P, what are three pairs of congruent triangles? © MP.7

EXAMPLE 3

Try It! Use a Circumcenter

3. In the illustration, point E represents where a new power generator can be built so that it is the same distance from the school, hospital, and recreation center. If the city manager decided to place the generator so that it is the same distance from the hospital, school, and grocery store, how can she find the location?

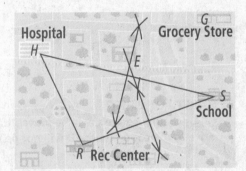

EXAMPLE 4

Try It! Investigate Inscribed Circles

4. Do you think the incenter of a triangle (the point of concurrency of the angle bisectors of a triangle) can ever be located on the side of the triangle? Explain.

HABITS OF MIND

Communicate Precisely Describe how the incenter and circumcenter of a triangle are alike and how they are different. © MP.6

EXAMPLE 5

Try It! Identify and Use the Incenter of a Triangle

5. Use the figure shown.

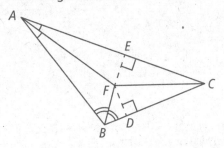

a. If $m\angle BAF = 15$ and $m\angle CBF = 52$, what is $m\angle ACF$?

b. If $EF = 3y - 5$ and $DF = 2y + 4$, what is the distance from F to $\overline{AB}$?

HABITS OF MIND

Construct Arguments For which triangles will the incenter and the circumcenter be the same point? Explain. © MP.3

Do You UNDERSTAND?

1. **ESSENTIAL QUESTION** What are the properties of the perpendicular bisectors in a triangle? What are the properties of the angle bisectors in a triangle?

2. **Error Analysis** Terrence constructed the circumscribed circle for △XYZ. Explain Terrence's error. © MP.3

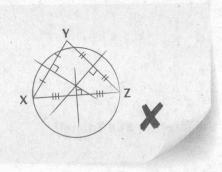

3. **Vocabulary** What parts of the triangle is the *circumcenter* equidistant from? What parts of the triangle is the *incenter* equidistant from?

4. **Reason** Is it possible for the circumscribed circle and the inscribed circle of a triangle to be the same? Explain your reasoning. © MP.2

Do You KNOW HOW?

The perpendicular bisectors of △ABC are $\overline{PT}$, $\overline{QT}$, and $\overline{RT}$. Find each length.

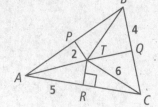

5. *AT*

6. *RC*

Two of the angle bisectors of △ABC are $\overline{AP}$ and $\overline{BP}$. Find each value.

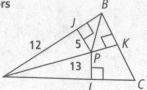

7. *PK*

8. Perimeter of △APL

9. An artist will place a circular piece of stained glass inside the triangular frame so that the glass touches each side of the frame. What is the diameter of the stained glass? Round to the nearest tenth.

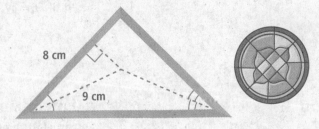

SavvasRealize.com

Making It Fair

In rural areas, county planners often work with local officials from a number of small towns to establish a regional medical center to serve all of the nearby communities.

County planners might also establish regional medical evacuation centers to transport patients with serious trauma to larger medical centers. The locations of these regional centers are carefully planned. Think about this during the Mathematical Modeling in 3 Acts lesson.

ACT 1 ▶ Identify the Problem

1. What is the first question that comes to mind after watching the video?

2. Write down the main question you will answer about what you saw in the video.

3. Make an initial conjecture that answers this main question.

4. Explain how you arrived at your conjecture.

5. What information will be useful to know to answer the main question? How can you get it? How will you use that information?

ACT 2 ▶ Develop a Model

6. Use the math that you have learned in this Topic to refine your conjecture.

ACT 3 ▶ Interpret the Results

7. Did your refined conjecture match the actual answer exactly? If not, what might explain the difference?

CRITIQUE & EXPLAIN

Aisha wrote the following explanation of the relationships in the triangle.

I can see that ∠TVY ≅ ∠YVU, ∠VUX ≅ ∠XUT, and ∠UTZ ≅ ∠ZTV because $\overline{TZ}$, $\overline{VY}$, and $\overline{UX}$ bisect the sides opposite each vertex. By the Concurrency of Angle Bisectors Theorem, $\overline{VY}$, $\overline{UX}$, and $\overline{TZ}$ are concurrent.

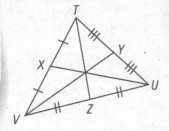

A. Why is Aisha's explanation not correct?

B. Communicate Precisely What can you do in the future to avoid Aisha's mistake? Ⓒ MP.6

HABITS OF MIND

Construct Arguments If △TUV were an equilateral triangle, would Aisha's assumption about angle congruencies be correct? Explain. Ⓒ MP.3

EXAMPLE 1

Try It! Identify Special Segments in Triangles

1. Use the figure shown.

   a. What are the altitude and median that are shown in △ABC?

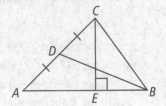

   b. Copy the triangle and draw the other altitudes and medians of the triangle.

HABITS OF MIND

Reason In △JKL, suppose $\overline{KP}$ is a median and an altitude. Is $\overline{KP}$ also a perpendicular bisector? Explain. © MP.2

EXAMPLE 2

Try It! Find the Length of a Median

2. Find AD for each triangle.

   a.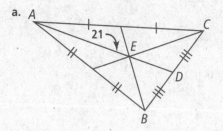

   b.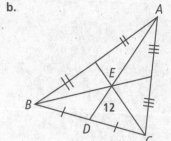

EXAMPLE 3

Try It! Locate the Centroid

3. For the triangle shown:

a. Use the medians of the triangle to locate its centroid.

b. Use a ruler to verify the centroid is two-thirds the distance from each vertex to the midpoint of the opposite side.

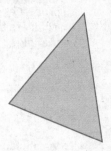

HABITS OF MIND

Use Structure If you are given a diagram showing two vertices and the centroid of a triangle, how could you locate the third vertex? © MP.7

EXAMPLE 4

Try It! Locate the Orthocenter

4. What is the relationship between an isosceles triangle and the location of its orthocenter (the point of concurrency of the lines containing the altitudes of a triangle)? Explain your answer.

EXAMPLE 5

Try It! Find the Orthocenter of a Triangle

5. Find the orthocenter of a triangle with vertices at each of the following sets of coordinates.

a. (0, 0), (10, 4), (8, 9)   b. (0, 0), (6, 3), (8, 9)

HABITS OF MIND

Construct Arguments A right triangle has vertices $X(0, 0)$, $Y(0, 2a)$, and $Z(2b, 0)$. Explain why the orthocenter of a right triangle is at the vertex of the right angle. © MP.3

Do You UNDERSTAND?

1. **ESSENTIAL QUESTION** What are the properties of the medians in a triangle? What are the properties of the altitudes in a triangle?

2. **Vocabulary** The prefix *ortho-* means "upright" or "right." How can this meaning help you remember which segments of a triangle have a point of concurrency at the orthocenter?

3. **Error Analysis** A student labeled *P* as the centroid of the triangle. What error did the student make? Explain. © MP.3

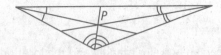

4. **Reason** Why is an orthocenter sometimes outside a triangle but a centroid is always inside? © MP.2

5. **Look for Relationships** Consider the three types of triangles: acute, obtuse, and right. What is the relationship between the type of triangle and the location of the orthocenter? Does the type of triangle tell you anything about the location of the centroid? © MP.7

6. **Generalize** For any right triangle, where is the orthocenter located? © MP.8

Do You KNOW HOW?

7. Find the length of each of the medians of the triangle.

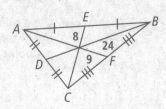

8. Where is the orthocenter of △*ABC*?

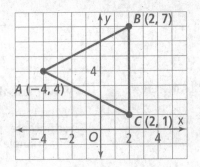

9. A crane operator needs to lift a large triangular piece of plywood. Copy the triangle and use its medians to locate the centroid.

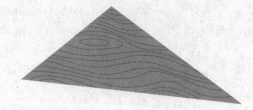

EXPLORE & REASON

Cut several drinking straws to the sizes shown.

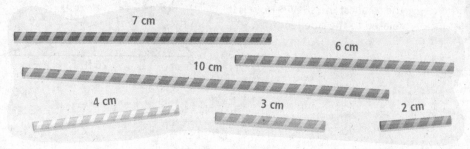

7 cm

6 cm

10 cm

4 cm

3 cm

2 cm

A. Take your two shortest straws and your longest straw. Can they form a triangle? Explain.

B. Try different combinations of three straws to form triangles. Which side length combinations work? Which combinations do not work?

C. Look for Relationships What do you notice about the relationship between the combined lengths of the two shorter sides and the length of the longest side? © MP.7

HABITS OF MIND

Look for Relationships A triangle has side lengths x, $x - 5$, and $x + 5$. Give a value of x that will work for this relationship. Explain. © MP.7

EXAMPLE 1

Try It! Investigate Side and Angle Relationships

1. Which angle measure appears to be the smallest in △MNP? How is it related to the side lengths?

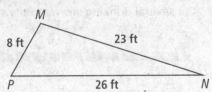

EXAMPLE 2

Try It! Use Theorem 5-9

2. Lucas sketched a diagram for a garden box.

   a. Which angle is the largest?

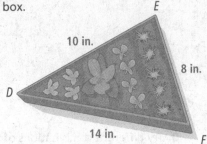

   b. Which angle is the smallest?

HABITS OF MIND

Generalize In △XYZ, XY < YZ < XZ. Write an inequality showing the relationship between the measures of the three angles of △XYZ. © MP.8

EXAMPLE 3

Try It! Prove Theorem 5-10

3. Theorem 5-10 states that if two angles of a triangle are not congruent, then the longer side lies opposite the larger angle. In the diagram, $m\angle J > m\angle G$. In an indirect proof of the theorem, assuming that $GH = HJ$ leads to a contradiction of the given condition $m\angle J > m\angle G$. To complete the proof, show that assuming $GH < HJ$ also leads to a contradiction of the given condition that $m\angle J > m\angle G$.

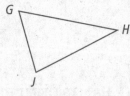

EXAMPLE 4

Try It! Use Theorem 5-10

4. Identify the sides of △NOP.

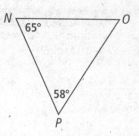

   a. Which side is the longest?

   b. Which side is the shortest?

HABITS OF MIND

Construct Arguments In any triangle with a 105° angle, is the longest side always opposite this angle? Explain. ⓒ **MP.3**

EXAMPLE 5

Try It! Use the Triangle Inequality Theorem

5. a. Could a triangle have side lengths 16 m, 39 m, and 28 m?

   b. A triangle has side lengths that are 30 in. and 50 in. What are the possible lengths of the third side?

HABITS OF MIND

Make Sense and Persevere If x is an integer and 2 < x < 8, how many triangles can be formed with side lengths 2, 8, and x? ⓒ **MP.1**

Do You UNDERSTAND?

1. **ESSENTIAL QUESTION** What are some relationships between the sides and angles of any triangle?

2. **Reason** If a triangle has three different side lengths, what does that tell you about the measures of its angles? © **MP.2**

3. **Error Analysis** Richard says that ∠X must be the largest angle in △XYZ. Explain his error. © **MP.3**

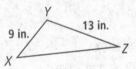

4. **Use Structure** An isosceles triangle has base angles that each measure 50. How could you determine whether b or s is greater? © **MP.7**

5. **Generalize** In △ABC, a < c < b. List the angles in order from smallest to largest. © **MP.8**

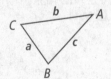

Do You KNOW HOW?

Identify the sides of △PQR.

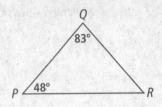

6. Which side is the longest?

7. Which side is the shortest?

Determine whether each set of lengths could form a triangle.

8. 5, 2, and 3

9. 55, 76, and 112

10. 102, 95, and 157

11. 17, 17, and 35

12. Kelsey is welding 3 metal rods to make a triangle. If the lengths of two of the rods are 15 in. and 22 in., what are the possible lengths of a third rod?

EXPLORE & REASON

A woodworker uses a caliper to measure the widths of a bat to help him determine the widths for a new bat. The woodworker places the open tips of the caliper on the bat. The distance between the tips is a width of the bat.

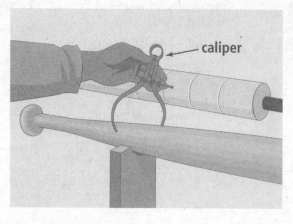

caliper

A. Suppose a caliper opens to an angle of 25° for one width of a bat and opens to an angle of 35° for another. What can you conclude about the widths of the bat?

B. Look for Relationships Next, suppose you use a caliper to measure the width of a narrow part of a bat and a wider part of the bat. What can you predict about the angle to which the caliper opens each time? © MP.7

HABITS OF MIND

Communicate Precisely Compare the caliper to a compass. If you open the compass to a wider angle, how does the relationship between the compass point and pencil point change? © MP.6

EXAMPLE 1

Try It! Investigate Side Lengths in Triangles

1. Compare the measures of the labeled angle and side lengths for the triangles.

acute   obtuse   right

EXAMPLE 2

Try It! Apply the Hinge Theorem

2. The diagram represents a person standing with his shoulders at *J*, hands at *L*, and feet at *K*. A tension band extends from *K* to *L*.

The person keeps his arms extended and the length of the tension band the same. If he wants to make the measure of ∠L smaller, how would the length of $\overline{JK}$, the vertical distance from the person's shoulders to his feet, change?

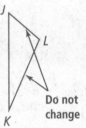

HABITS OF MIND

Look for Relationships How are applying the Hinge Theorem and SAS Theorem alike and different? © MP.7

EXAMPLE 3

Try It! Prove the Converse of the Hinge Theorem

3. The Converse of the Hinge Theorem states that if two sides of one triangle are congruent to two sides of another triangle, and the third sides are not congruent, then the larger included angle is opposite the longer third side.

In the diagram, $EF > UV$. In an indirect proof of the Converse of the Hinge Theorem, assume that $m\angle FDE = m\angle VTU$ leads to a contradiction of the given statement $EF > UV$. To complete the proof, show that assuming $m\angle FDE < m\angle VTU$ also leads to a contradiction of the given statement, $EF > UV$.

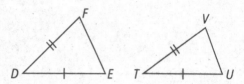

EXAMPLE 4

Try It! Apply the Converse of the Hinge Theorem

4. What are the possible values of x for each diagram?

a.

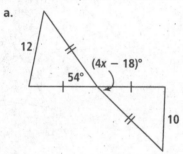

b.

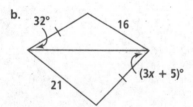

HABITS OF MIND

Make Sense and Persevere Explain the Converse of the Hinge Theorem using the triangle formed by the unicycle seat post, crank arm, and segment connecting the seat post with the pedal from Example 1, shown below. ⓒ MP.1

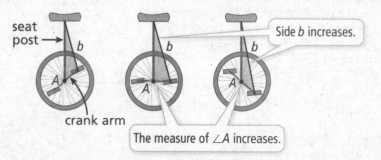

seat post → b
crank arm
Side b increases.
The measure of ∠A increases.

Do You UNDERSTAND?

1. **ESSENTIAL QUESTION** When two triangles have two pairs of congruent sides, how are the third pair of sides and the pair of angles opposite the third pair of sides related?

2. **Error Analysis** Venetta applies the Converse of the Hinge Theorem to conclude that $m\angle EKF > m\angle HKG$ for the triangles shown. Is Venetta correct? Explain your answer. © MP.3

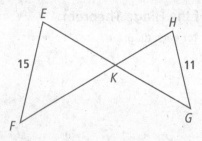

3. **Reason** Why must the angles described in the Hinge Theorem be between the congruent pairs of sides? © MP.2

4. **Communicate Precisely** The Hinge Theorem is also known as the Side-Angle-Side Inequality Theorem or SAS Inequality Theorem. How are the requirements for applying the Hinge Theorem similar to the requirements for applying SAS? How are the requirements different? © MP.6

Do You KNOW HOW?

5. Order AB, BC, and CD from least to greatest.

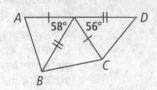

6. Order the measures of $\angle PTU$, $\angle SQT$, and $\angle QSR$ from least to greatest.

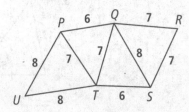

7. Kayak A and kayak B leave a dock as shown. Which kayak is closer to the dock?

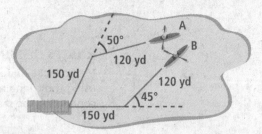

EXPLORE & REASON

Start by drawing a pentagon. Then, for each side of the pentagon, draw a line that includes the side. An example is shown.

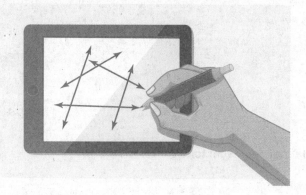

SavvasRealize.com

A. Choose one pair of lines that intersect at a vertex of the pentagon. Is each of the four angles formed at the vertex an interior angle or an exterior angle of the pentagon?

B. Are the relationships the same for the angles formed by the other pairs of intersecting lines?

C. Make Sense and Persevere If you drew a hexagon and the lines that included the sides of the hexagon, would the relationships between the angles at each vertex be the same as those in the pentagon? © MP.1

HABITS OF MIND

Communicate Precisely What mathematical definitions can you use to describe the relationships among the angles in the diagram? © MP.6

EXAMPLE 1

Try It! Explore Polygon Interior Angle Sums

1. a. How many triangles are formed by drawing diagonals from a vertex in a convex octagon?

   b. What is the interior angle sum for a convex octagon?

EXAMPLE 2

Try It! Apply the Polygon Interior Angle-Sum Theorem

2. a. What is the interior angle sum of a 17-gon?

   b. Each angle of a regular n-gon measures 172.8. How many sides does the n-gon have?

HABITS OF MIND

Use Appropriate Tools Would drawing a diagram or using the formula be more helpful in finding the interior angle sum of an n-gon with more than 10 sides? Explain. © MP.5

EXAMPLE 3

Try It! Understand Exterior Angle Measures of a Polygon

3. What is the sum of exterior angle measures of a convex 17-gon?

EXAMPLE 4

Try It! Find an Exterior Angle Measure

4. Suppose $\angle 1 \cong \angle 3 \cong \angle 4 \cong \angle 6$, $\angle 2 \cong \angle 5$, and $m\angle 3 = m\angle 2 + 30$. What is $m\angle 4$?

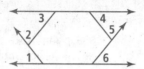

EXAMPLE 5

Try It! Find the Measures of Interior Angles

5. The measure of each interior angle of a regular 100-gon is $(3x + 26.4)$. What is the value of x?

HABITS OF MIND

Generalize Under what circumstances would you *not* want to divide the interior angle sum of a polygon by the number of sides? Ⓒ **MP.8**

Do You UNDERSTAND?

1. **ESSENTIAL QUESTION** How does the number of sides in convex polygons relate to the sums of the measures of the exterior and interior angles?

2. **Error Analysis** In the calculation shown, what is Valeria's error? © MP.3

> The sum of the measures of the exterior angles of a 25-gon is
> $180 \cdot (25 - 2) = 4{,}140$. ✗

3. **Make Sense and Persevere** What is the minimum amount of information needed to find the sum of the interior angles of a regular polygon? © MP.1

4. **Reason** A convex polygon can be decomposed into 47 triangles. How many sides does the polygon have? Explain. © MP.2

Do You KNOW HOW?

Use Polygon A for Exercises 5 and 6.

Polygon A

5. What is the sum of the measures of the interior angles?

6. What is the sum of the measures of the exterior angles?

Use Polygon B for Exercises 7 and 8.

7. What is the value of y?

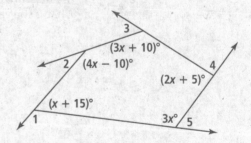

Polygon B

8. What is the value of x?

9. What are the measures of the exterior angles of the polygon shown?

3
$(3x + 10)°$
2 $(4x - 10)°$
4
$(2x + 5)°$
$(x + 15)°$
1
$3x°$ 5

10. The sum of the interior angles of a regular n-gon is 6,120. What is the measure of each interior angle?

MATHEMATICAL
MODELING
IN **3** ACTS

The Mystery Sides

Have you ever looked closely at honeycombs? What shape are they? How do you know? Most often the cells in the honeycombs look like hexagons, but they might also look like circles. Scientists now believe that bees make circular cells that become hexagonal due to the bees' body heat and natural physical forces.

What are some strategies you use to identify shapes? Think about this during the Mathematical Modeling in 3 Acts lesson.

ACT 1 ▶ Identify the Problem

1. What is the first question that comes to mind after watching the video?

2. Write down the main question you will answer about what you saw in the video.

3. Make an initial conjecture that answers this main question.

4. Explain how you arrived at your conjecture.

5. What information will be useful to know to answer the main question? How can you get it? How will you use that information?

ACT 2 Develop a Model

6. Use the math that you have learned in this Topic to refine your conjecture.

ACT 3 Interpret the Results

7. Did your refined conjecture match the actual answer exactly? If not, how is it different? What might explain the difference?

CRITIQUE & EXPLAIN

Manuel is designing kite-shaped key chains for the Debate Team. He draws kite *PQRS* with $\overleftrightarrow{QS}$ as the line of symmetry. He makes a list of conclusions based on the diagram.

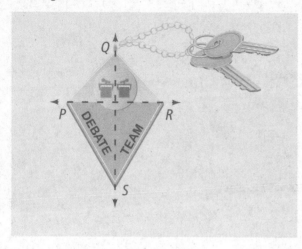

- $\overline{PR} \perp \overline{QS}$
- $\overline{QP} \cong \overline{QR}$
- $\overline{SP} \cong \overline{SR}$
- $\overline{PR}$ bisects $\overline{QS}$.
- $\triangle PQR$ is an equilateral triangle.
- $\triangle PSR$ is an isosceles triangle.

A. Which of Manuel's conclusions do you agree with? Which do you disagree with? Explain.

B. Use Structure What other conclusions are supported by the diagram? © **MP.7**

HABITS OF MIND

Construct Arguments What theorems or definitions support your conclusions?
© **MP.3**

EXAMPLE 1

Try It! Investigate the Diagonals of a Kite

1. a. What is the measure of ∠AXB?

b. If AX = 3.8, what is AC?

c. If BD = 10, does BX = 5? Explain.

EXAMPLE 2

Try It! Use the Diagonals of a Kite

2. Quadrilateral WXYZ is a kite.

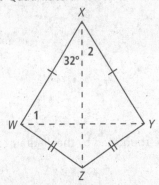

a. What is m∠1?

b. What is m∠2?

- - - - - - - - - - - - - - - - - - - -

HABITS OF MIND

Use Structure What ideas about triangles have you learned that could be useful in investigating kites? ⒸMP.7

EXAMPLE 3

Try It! **Explore Parts of an Isosceles Trapezoid**

3. **a.** Given isosceles trapezoid *PQRS*, what are $m\angle P$, $m\angle Q$, and $m\angle S$?

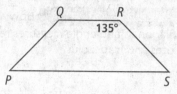

b. Given $\overline{ST} \parallel \overline{RU}$, what is the measure of $\angle TUR$?

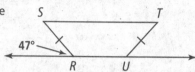

EXAMPLE 4

Try It! **Solve Problems Involving Isosceles Trapezoids**

4. Given isosceles trapezoid *MNOP* where the given expressions represent the measures of the diagonals, what is the value of *a*?

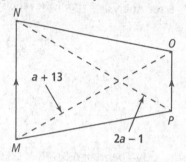

HABITS OF MIND

Make Sense and Persevere What is the minimum amount of information you need to find the measures of all four interior angles in an isosceles trapezoid? ⓒ **MP.1**

EXAMPLE 5

Try It! **Apply the Trapezoid Midsegment Theorem**

5. Given trapezoid *JKLM*, what is *KL*?

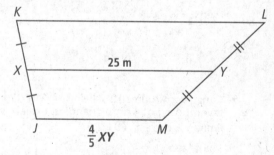

HABITS OF MIND

Communicate Precisely What information is represented in the diagram but not given in words in the problem statement? ⓒ **MP.6**

Do You UNDERSTAND?

1. **ESSENTIAL QUESTION** How are diagonals and angle measures related in kites and trapezoids?

2. **Error Analysis** What is Nevaeh's error? © MP.3

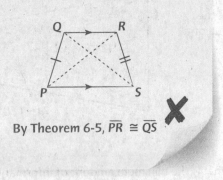

By Theorem 6-5, $\overline{PR} \cong \overline{QS}$ ✗

3. **Vocabulary** If $\overline{XY}$ is the midsegment of a trapezoid, what must be true about point X and point Y?

4. **Construct Arguments** Emaan says every kite is composed of 4 right triangles. Explain why Emaan is correct. © MP.3

Do You KNOW HOW?

For Exercises 5–7, use kite *WXYZ* to find the measures.

5. $m\angle XQY$

6. $m\angle YZQ$

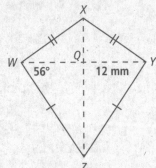

7. *WY*

For Exercises 8–10, use trapezoid *DEFG* with $EG = 21$ ft and $m\angle DGF = 77°$ to find each measure.

8. *ED*

9. *DF*

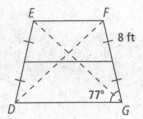

10. $m\angle DEF$

11. What is the length of $\overline{PQ}$?

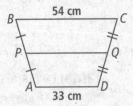

CRITIQUE & EXPLAIN

Kennedy lists all the pairs of congruent triangles she finds in quadrilateral *ABCD*.

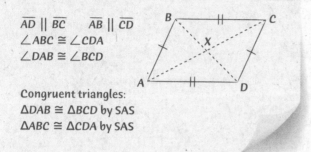

$\overline{AD} \parallel \overline{BC}$ $\overline{AB} \parallel \overline{CD}$
$\angle ABC \cong \angle CDA$
$\angle DAB \cong \angle BCD$

Congruent triangles:
$\triangle DAB \cong \triangle BCD$ by SAS
$\triangle ABC \cong \triangle CDA$ by SAS

A. Is Kennedy's justification for triangle congruence correct for each pair?

B. Look for Relationships Did Kennedy overlook any pairs of congruent triangles? If not, explain how you know. If so, name them and explain how you know they are congruent. **MP.7**

HABITS OF MIND

Make Sense and Persevere Why might it be useful to start analyzing a parallelogram by decomposing it into triangles? **MP.1**

EXAMPLE 1

Try It! Explore Opposite Sides of Parallelograms

1. Given parallelogram *WXYZ*, what is *YZ*?

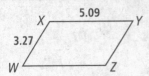

EXAMPLE 2

Try It! Use Opposite Sides of a Parallelogram

2. The 600-meter fence around City Park forms a parallelogram. The fence along Chaco Road is twice as long as the fence along Grover Lane. What is the length of the fence along Jones Road?

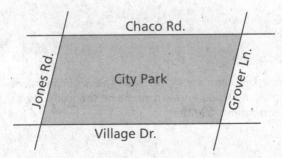

- -

HABITS OF MIND

Use Structure If you know the perimeter of a parallelogram, what information would you need to know in order to determine the lengths of the sides? Ⓒ **MP.7**

✎ Notes

EXAMPLE 3

Try It! Explore Angle Measures in Parallelograms

3. a. Given parallelogram *ABCD*, what are $m\angle A$ and $m\angle C$?

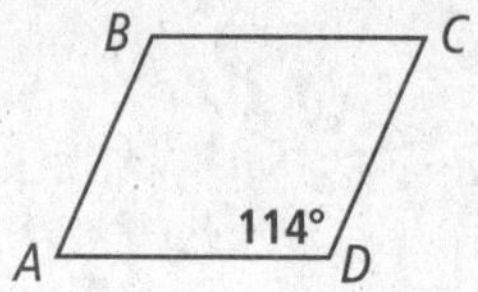

a. What is $m\angle B$?

Notes

EXAMPLE 4

Try It! Use Angles of a Parallelogram

4. Use the parallelogram shown.

   a. Given parallelogram *GHJK*, what is the value of *a*?

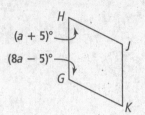

   b. What are $m\angle G$, $m\angle H$, $m\angle J$, and $m\angle K$?

HABITS OF MIND

Reason Under what conditions can a pair of consecutive angles in a parallelogram be congruent? Explain. © MP.2

144 TOPIC 6 Quadrilaterals and Other Polygons

EXAMPLE 5

Try It! Explore the Diagonals of a Parallelogram

5. Use parallelogram *RSTU* with *SU* = 35 and *KT* = 19.

   a. What is *SK*?

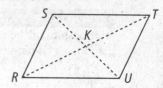

   b. What is *RT*?

EXAMPLE 6

Try It! Find Unknown Lengths in a Parallelogram

6. Given parallelogram *GHJK* if *PK* = 4 and $HK = \frac{2}{3}(GJ)$, what is *GP*?

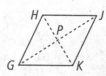

HABITS OF MIND

Look for Relationships How can you tell which diagonal of a parallelogram has the greater length? © **MP.7**

Do You UNDERSTAND?

1. **ESSENTIAL QUESTION** What are the relationships of the sides, the angles, and the diagonals of a parallelogram?

2. **Error Analysis** What is Pablo's error? © MP.3

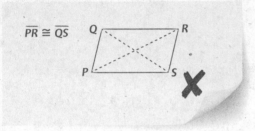

$\overline{PR} \cong \overline{QS}$

3. **Make Sense and Persevere** If you knew the length of $\overline{DF}$ in parallelogram *DEFG*, how would you find the length of $\overline{DK}$? Explain. © MP.1

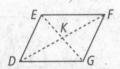

4. **Reason** Given parallelogram *JKLM*, what could the expression $180 - (3x + 8)$ represent? Explain. © MP.2

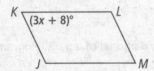

Do You KNOW HOW?

For Exercises 5 and 6, use parallelogram *ABCD* to find each length. The length of $\overline{DE}$ is $x + 2$.

5. *BC*

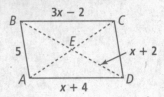

6. *BD*

For Exercises 7 and 8, use parallelogram *WXYZ* to find each angle measure.

7. $m\angle WXY$

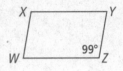

8. $m\angle XYZ$

For Exercises 9 and 10, use parallelogram *EFGH* to find each length.

9. *EJ*

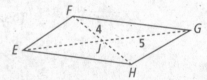

10. *FH*

For Exercises 11 and 12, use parallelogram *MNPQ* to find each angle measure.

11. $m\angle NPQ$

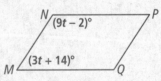

12. $m\angle PQM$

EXPLORE & REASON

Sketch the quadrilaterals as described in the table. Include the diagonals.

	Parallel Sides	Congruent Sides
Quadrilateral 1	0 pairs	2 consecutive pairs
Quadrilateral 2	1 pair	exactly 1 non-parallel pair
Quadrilateral 3	2 pairs	2 opposite pairs

A. Measure the angles of each quadrilateral. How are the angle measures in Quadrilateral 1 related to each other? in Quadrilateral 2? in Quadrilateral 3?

B. Measure the diagonals of each quadrilateral. How are the diagonals in Quadrilateral 1 related to each other? in Quadrilateral 2? in Quadrilateral 3?

C. Communicate Precisely Compare the relationships among the angles and diagonals of Quadrilateral 3 to the other two quadrilaterals. Are there any relationships that make Quadrilateral 3 unique? ⓒ MP.6

HABITS OF MIND

Use Appropriate Tools How might a geoboard be helpful in comparing quadrilaterals? ⓒ MP.5

EXAMPLE 1

Try It! Investigate Sides to Confirm a Parallelogram

1. Explain why you cannot conclude that *ABCD* is a parallelogram.

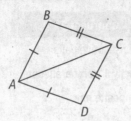

HABITS OF MIND

Use Structure Suppose a scalene triangle is reflected across its longest side. Does the triangle combined with its image form a parallelogram? Explain.
© MP.7

EXAMPLE 2

Try It! Explore Angle Measures to Confirm a Parallelogram

2. a. Is *DEFG* a parallelogram? Explain.

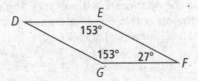

b. Is *LMNO* a parallelogram? Explain.

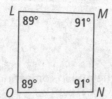

EXAMPLE 3

Try It! Find Values to Make Parallelograms.

3. a. If $x = 25$ and $y = 30$, is *PQRS* a parallelogram?

b. If $g = 14$ and $h = 5$, is *ABCD* a parallelogram?

HABITS OF MIND

Reason Given algebraic expressions for the angles of a quadrilateral, what properties could you use to decide if the quadrilateral is a parallelogram?
Ⓒ MP.2

EXAMPLE 4

Try It! Investigate Diagonals to Confirm a Parallelogram

4. For what values of p and q is $ABCD$ a parallelogram?

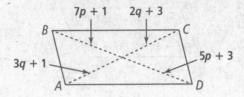

EXAMPLE 5

Try It! Identify a Parallelogram

5. a. Is $ABCD$ a parallelogram? Explain.

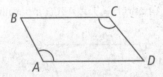

   b. Is $EFGH$ a parallelogram? Explain.

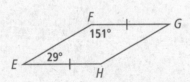

HABITS OF MIND

Reason Given algebraic expressions for the diagonals of a quadrilateral, what properties could you use to decide if the quadrilateral is a parallelogram?
Ⓒ MP.2

EXAMPLE 6

Try It! Verify a Parallelogram

6. A carpenter builds the table shown. If the floor is level, how likely is it that a ball placed on the table will roll off?

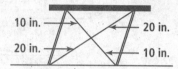

10 in.   20 in.

20 in.   10 in.

HABITS OF MIND

Make Sense and Persevere How would you describe this problem in your own words? © MP.1

Do You UNDERSTAND?

1. **ESSENTIAL QUESTION** Which properties determine whether a quadrilateral is a parallelogram?

2. Error Analysis Explain why Rochelle is incorrect. © MP.3

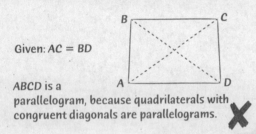

Given: $AC = BD$

ABCD is a parallelogram, because quadrilaterals with congruent diagonals are parallelograms.

3. Make Sense and Persevere Is the information in the diagram enough to show WXYZ is a parallelogram? Explain. © MP.1

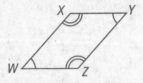

Do You KNOW HOW?

What must each angle measure be in order for quadrilateral DEFG to be a parallelogram?

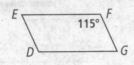

4. $m\angle D$ **5.** $m\angle E$

What must each length be in order for quadrilateral JKLM to be a parallelogram?

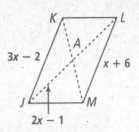

6. JK   **7.** JL

Use the diagram for Exercises 8 and 9.

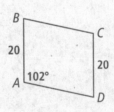

8. If $\overline{AB} \parallel \overline{DC}$, is ABCD a parallelogram? Explain.

9. If ABCD is a parallelogram, how does AC compare to BD? Explain.

EXPLORE & REASON

Consider these three figures.

Figure 1   Figure 2   Figure 3

A. What questions would you ask to determine whether each figure is a parallelogram?

B. Communicate Precisely What questions would you ask to determine whether Figure 1 is a rectangle? What questions would you ask to determine whether Figure 2 is a square? © **MP.6**

C. If all three figures are parallelograms, what is the most descriptive name for Figure 3? How do you know?

- -

HABITS OF MIND

Construct Arguments What do you use and look for to classify a figure? © **MP.3**

EXAMPLE 1

Try It! Investigate the Angles Formed by the Diagonals of a Rhombus

1. a. What is WY?

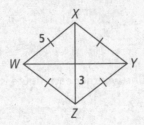

b. What is m∠RPS?

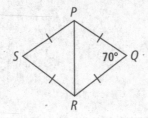

EXAMPLE 2

Try It! Find Lengths and Angle Measures in a Rhombus

2. Each quadrilateral is a rhombus.

a. What is m∠MNO?

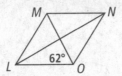

b. What is QT?

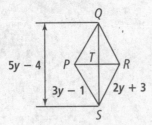

HABITS OF MIND

Use Structure Consider the relationships of the triangles in a rhombus. When solving problems involving a rhombus, what types of theorems do you think will be useful? Ⓒ MP.7

EXAMPLE 3

Try It! Prove Diagonals of a Rectangle Are Congruent

3. A carpenter needs to check the gate his apprentice built to be sure it is rectangular. The diagonals measure 52 inches and 53 inches. Is the gate rectangular? Explain.

EXAMPLE 4

Try It! Find Diagonal Lengths of a Rectangle

4. A rectangle with area 1,600 m^2 is 4 times as long as it is wide. What is the sum of the diagonals?

EXAMPLE 5

Try It! Diagonals and Angle Measures of a Square

5. Square $ABCD$ has diagonals $\overline{AC}$ and $\overline{BD}$. What is $m\angle ABD$? Explain.

HABITS OF MIND

Generalize How do the parallelograms whose diagonals are congruent compare to those whose diagonals are not congruent? © MP.8

Do You UNDERSTAND?

1. **ESSENTIAL QUESTION** What properties of rhombuses, rectangles, and squares differentiate them from other parallelograms?

2. **Error Analysis** Figure *QRST* is a rectangle. Ramona wants to show that the four interior triangles are congruent. What is Ramona's error? © MP.3

Diagonals of a rectangle are congruent and bisect each other, so $\overline{RP} \cong \overline{TP} \cong \overline{QP} \cong \overline{SP}$. Because the diagonals are perpendicular bisectors, $\angle RPS$, $\angle SPT$, $\angle TPQ$, and $\angle QPR$ are right angles. Therefore, by SAS,

$\triangle RPS \cong \triangle SPT \cong \triangle TPQ \cong \triangle PQR.$ ✗

3. **Construct Arguments** Is any quadrilateral with four congruent sides a rhombus? Explain. © MP.3

Do You KNOW HOW?

Find each length and angle measure for rhombus *DEFG*. Round to the nearest tenth.

4. *DF*

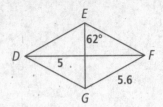

5. m∠*DFG*

6. *EG*

Find each length for rectangle *MNPQ*. Round to the nearest tenth.

7. *MP*

8. *MQ*

Find each length and angle measure for square *WXYZ*.

9. m∠*YPZ*

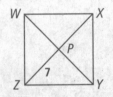

10. m∠*XWP*

11. *XZ*

12. What is the value of *x*?

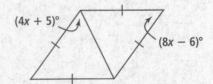

$(4x + 5)°$ $(8x − 6)°$

MODEL & DISCUSS

Floating lanterns both in the sky and on water are rooted in ancient cultural traditions. Today, they are used to commemorate cultural and spiritual celebrations across Asia and the US. The sides of the water lantern shown are identical quadrilaterals.

A. Construct Arguments How could you check to see whether a side is a parallelogram? Justify your answer. © MP.3

B. Does the side appear to be rectangular? How could you check?

C. Do you think that diagonals of a quadrilateral can be used to determine whether the quadrilateral is a rectangle? Explain.

HABITS OF MIND

Use Structure What ideas have you previously learned that might suggest that squares, rhombuses, and rectangles can be identified using their diagonals? © MP.7

EXAMPLE 1

Try It! Use Diagonals to Identify Rhombuses

1. If ∠JHK and ∠JGK are complementary, what else can you conclude about GHJK? Explain.

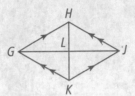

EXAMPLE 2

Try It! Prove Theorem 6-20

2. Use properties of parallelograms to show that if ∠1 ≅ ∠2 and ∠3 ≅ ∠4, then the four angles are congruent.

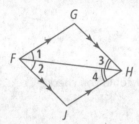

HABITS OF MIND

Construct Arguments Theorem 6-19 states, "If the diagonals of a parallelogram are perpendicular, then the parallelogram is a rhombus." Theorem 6-20 states, "If a diagonal of a parallelogram bisects two angles of the parallelogram, then the parallelogram is a rhombus." Why do you think these theorems state that the figure must be a parallelogram? © MP.3

EXAMPLE 3

Try It! Use Diagonals to Identify Rectangles

3. If the diagonals of any quadrilateral are congruent, is the quadrilateral a rectangle? Justify your answer.

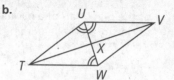

EXAMPLE 4

Try It! Identify Special Parallelograms

4. Is each parallelogram a rhombus, a square, or a rectangle? Explain.

a.

b.

EXAMPLE 5

Try It! Use Properties of Special Parallelograms

5. In parallelogram *ABCD*, *AC* = 3*w* − 1 and *BD* = 2(*w* + 6). What must be true for *ABCD* to be a rectangle?

EXAMPLE 6

Try It! Apply Properties of Special Parallelograms

6. Is *MNPQ* a rhombus? Explain.

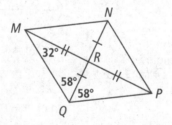

- -

HABITS OF MIND

Use Structure In what ways does showing that a parallelogram is a special parallelogram connect to other mathematical concepts? ©️ **MP.7**

Do You UNDERSTAND?

1. **ESSENTIAL QUESTION** Which properties of the diagonals of a parallelogram help you to classify a parallelogram?

2. **Error Analysis** Sergio was asked to classify *DEFG*. What was Sergio's error? © MP.3

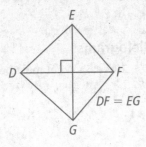

$DF = EG$

Since $DF = EG$, *DEFG* is a rectangle.
Since $\overline{EG} \perp \overline{DF}$, *DEFG* is also a rhombus.
Therefore, *DEFG* is a square.

✗

3. **Construct Arguments** Write a biconditional statement about the diagonals of rectangles. What theorems justify your statement? © MP.3

4. **Use Appropriate Tools** Make a concept map showing the relationships among quadrilaterals, parallelograms, trapezoids, isosceles trapezoids, kites, rectangles, squares, and rhombuses. © MP.5

Do You KNOW HOW?

For Exercises 5–8, is the parallelogram a rhombus, a square, or a rectangle?

5.

6.

7.

8.

9. What value of *x* will make the parallelogram a rhombus?

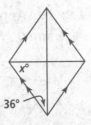

$x°$

$36°$

10. If $m\angle 1 = 36$ and $m\angle 2 = 54$, is *PQRS* a rhombus, a square, a rectangle, or none of these? Explain.

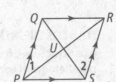

EXPLORE & REASON

Roosevelt High School sells a sticker and a larger car decal with the school logo.

A. **Look for Relationships** How are the sticker and the car decal alike? How are they different? Ⓒ MP.7

B. Suppose the sticker and decal are shown next to each other on a computer screen. If you zoom in to 125%, what would stay the same on the figures? What would be different?

HABITS OF MIND

Generalize What must be true about two figures that are the same shape but different sizes? Ⓒ MP.8

EXAMPLE 1

Try It! Dilate a Figure

1. a. Use The Ratio Method to dilate △*JKL* by a scale factor of 3 with center of dilation *R*.

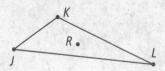

b. Use The Parallel Method to dilate △*PQR* by a scale factor of $\frac{1}{3}$ with center of dilation *M*.

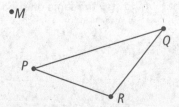

EXAMPLE 2

Try It! Analyze Dilations

2. Rectangle *W'X'Y'Z'* is a dilation with center *P* of *WXYZ*. How are the side lengths and angle measures of the two figures related?

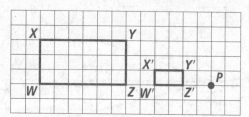

EXAMPLE 3

Try It! Find a Scale Factor

3. Consider the dilation shown.

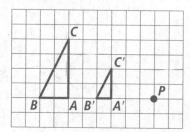

a. Is △*A'B'C'* an enlargement or a reduction of △*ABC*?

b. What is the scale factor?

HABITS OF MIND

Generalize In what ways are dilations similar to rotations, reflections, and translations? In what ways are they different? Ⓒ MP.8

EXAMPLE 4

Try It! **Dilate a Figure With Center at the Origin**

4. Use △*PQR*.

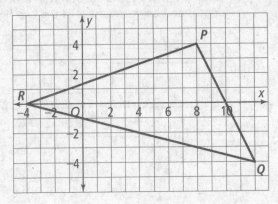

a. What are the vertices of D$\frac{1}{4}$(△*PQR*)?

b. How can you express the dilation algebraically?

c. How are the distances to the origin from each image point related to the distance to the origin from each corresponding preimage point?

EXAMPLE 5

Try It! Dilate a Figure With Center Not at the Origin

5. What are the vertices of $D_{(\frac{3}{2}, A)}$ (ABC)?

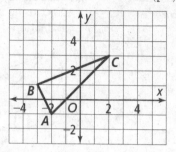

EXAMPLE 6

Try It! Solve Population Density Problems

6. Mott County is a rectangular region with dimensions 39 mi by 48 mi. Within Mott County, the town of Westville is a dilation of the county with scale factor $\frac{1}{2}$ and a population of 84,106. What is its population density?

HABITS OF MIND

Reason What is the same and what is different about dilations on the coordinate plane and dilations used in application problems? © MP.2

Do You UNDERSTAND?

1. How does a dilation affect the side lengths and angle measures of a figure?

2. **Error Analysis** Emilia was asked to find the coordinates of $D_2(\triangle ABC)$ for $A(2, 4)$, $B(0, 5)$, and $C(-2, 1)$. What is Emilia's error? © **MP.3**

$$A(2, 4) \rightarrow A'(4, 6)$$
$$B(0, 5) \rightarrow B'(2, 7)$$
$$C(-2, 1) \rightarrow C'(0, 3)$$

✗

3. **Vocabulary** In the definition of a dilation D_n, why can't n be equal to 0? What would a transformation like D_0 look like?

4. **Construct Arguments** Compare the vertices of $D_1(\triangle ABC)$ for any points A, B, and C. Justify your answer. © **MP.3**

Do You KNOW HOW?

5. Trace $\triangle JKL$ and point P. Draw the dilation of $\triangle JKL$ using scale factor 3 and P as the center of dilation.

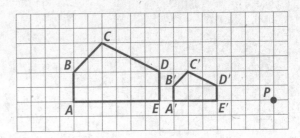

6. What is the scale factor for the dilation?

7. $(x, y) \rightarrow (5x, 5y)$ for $P(1, -3)$, $Q(-5, -4)$, $R(6, 2)$

Give the coordinates of the dilation.

8. $D_{(3, B)}(\triangle ABC)$ for $A(0, 4)$, $B(0, 2)$, $C(-3, 2)$

9. $D_{(4, F)}(FGHJ)$ for $F(0, -1)$, $G(4, -1)$, $H(4, -3)$, $J(0, -3)$

CRITIQUE & EXPLAIN

Helena and Edwin were asked to apply a composition of transformations to ABCD, as shown here.

Helena

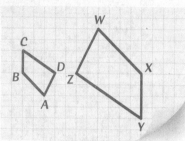

Edwin

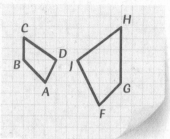

A. **Use Appropriate Tools** Is there a composition of transformations that maps ABCD to the second figure in each student's work? If so, what is it? © **MP.5**

B. For each student whose work shows a composition of transformations, describe the relationship between the figures.

HABITS OF MIND

Reason Given the preimage and image, how do you decide what transformations are used to create the image? © **MP.2**

EXAMPLE 1

Try It! Graph a Composition of a Rigid Motion and a Dilation

1. The vertices of $\triangle XYZ$ are $X(3, 5)$, $Y(-1, 4)$, and $Z(1, 7)$.

   a. What is the graph of the image $(D_2 \circ T_{\langle 1, -2 \rangle})(\triangle XYZ)$?

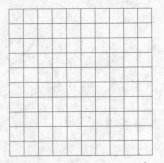

   b. What is the graph of the image $(D_3 \circ R_{(90°, O)})(\triangle XYZ)$?

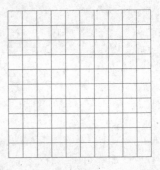

EXAMPLE 2

Try It! Describe a Composition of a Rigid Motion and a Dilation

2. $\triangle XYZ$ has vertices at points $(2,1)$, $(1,4)$ and $(4,1)$ respectively, whereas $\triangle JKL$ has vertices at the points $(-4,-2)$, $(-2, -8)$, and $(-8, -2)$ respectively. The composition of transformations $D_2 \circ R_{(180°, O)}$ maps $\triangle XYZ$ to $\triangle JKL$. If the transformations are performed in reverse order, are the results the same? Do you think your answer holds for all compositions of transformations? Explain.

HABITS OF MIND

Make Sense and Persevere Do you think there is a composition using different transformations that could produce the same image? Explain. © MP.1

EXAMPLE 3

Try It! Find Similarity Transformations

3. Describe a possible similarity transformation for each pair of similar figures shown, and then write a similarity statement.

a.

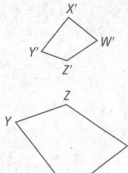

b.

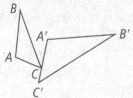

EXAMPLE 4

Try It! Determine Similarity

4. An artist cuts 2 inches from the width of a sketch measuring 11 in high and 14 in wide. She wants to copy her sketch to cover an entire wall measuring 15 ft high and 20 ft wide. How much should she cut from the height so she can copy a similar image to cover the wall?

- -

HABITS OF MIND

Communicate Precisely If two figures are congruent, are they also similar? If two figures are similar, are they also congruent? Explain. ⓒ MP.6

EXAMPLE 5

Try It! Identify Similar Circles

5. Write a proof that any two squares are similar.

- -

HABITS OF MIND

Make Sense and Persevere What are some other types of figures that are always similar to each other? Can you use a proof similar to the one proving two circles are similar to show they are always similar? Explain. ⓒ MP.1

Do You UNDERSTAND?

1. **ESSENTIAL QUESTION** What makes a transformation a similarity transformation? What is the relationship between a preimage and the image resulting from a similarity transformation?

2. **Error Analysis** Risa described the similarity transformation that maps △ABC to △XZY. What is Risa's error? © MP.3

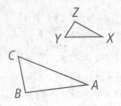

△ABC is dilated and then rotated to produce the image △XZY. ✗

3. **Vocabulary** How are similarity transformations and congruence transformations alike? How are they different?

4. **Construct Arguments** A similarity transformation consisting of a reflection and a dilation is performed on a figure, and one point maps to itself. Describe one way this could happen. © MP.3

Do You KNOW HOW?

For Exercises 5 and 6, what are the vertices of each image?

5. $R_{(90°, O)} \circ D_{0.5}(ABCD)$ for A(5, 1), B(−3, 4), C(0, 2), D(4, 6)

6. $(D_3 \circ r_{x\text{-axis}})(\triangle GHJ)$ for G(3, 5), H(1, −2), J(−1, 6)

7. Describe a similarity transformation that maps △SQR to △DEF.

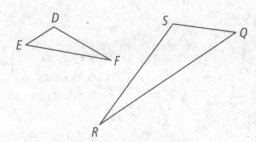

8. Do the two figures appear to be similar? Use transformations to explain.

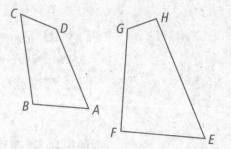

EXPLORE & REASON

The measurements of two triangles are shown.

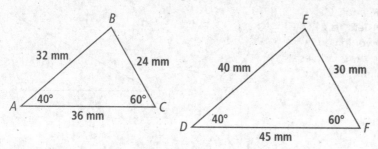

A. Are the triangles similar? Explain.

B. Construct Arguments Would any triangle with 40°- and 60°-angles be similar to △ABC? Explain. © **MP.3**

HABITS OF MIND

Make Sense and Persevere How can you use transformations to show that two triangles are similar? © **MP.1**

EXAMPLE 1

Try It! Establish the Angle-Angle Similarity (AA ~) Theorem

1. If ∠A is congruent to ∠R, and ∠C is congruent to ∠T, how would you prove the triangles are similar?

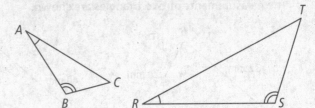

EXAMPLE 2

Try It! Establish the Side-Side-Side Similarity (SSS ~) Theorem

2. If $\frac{DF}{GJ} = \frac{EF}{HJ}$ and ∠F ≅ ∠J, is there a similarity transformation that maps △DEF to △GHJ? Explain.

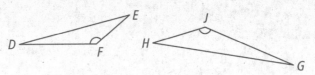

EXAMPLE 3

Try It! Verify Triangle Similarity

3. a. Is △ADE ~ △ABD? Explain.

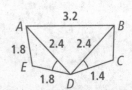

b. Is △ADE ~ △BDC? Explain.

- -

HABITS OF MIND

Make Sense and Persevere What steps would you take to determine if there is enough information to show that two triangles are similar? ⓒ MP.1

EXAMPLE 4

Try It! Find Lengths in Similar Triangles

4. a. The measure of *JL* is 150, *JK* is 10, and *LM* is 1. What is the measure of *MN*?

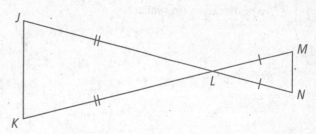

b. If the measure of *JL* is 75, *LM* is 1, and *JK* is 20, what is the value of *MN*?

EXAMPLE 5

Try It! Solve Problems Involving Similar Triangles

5. Avery is 6 ft tall and casts a shadow of 5 ft. If she installs an antenna tower that is 39 ft tall, how long would the shadow of the tower be?

HABITS OF MIND

Generalize How do you find an unknown length given a pair of similar triangles? ⓒ MP.8

Do You UNDERSTAND?

1. **ESSENTIAL QUESTION** How can you use the angles and sides of two triangles to determine whether they are similar?

2. **Error Analysis** Allie says △JKL ~ △XYZ. What is Allie's error? © MP.3

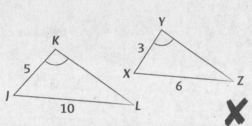

△JKL ~ △XYZ by the SAS ~ Theorem.

3. **Make Sense and Persevere** Is any additional information needed to show △DEF ~ △RST? Explain. © MP.1

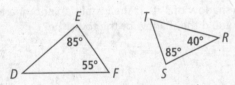

4. **Construct Arguments** Explain how you can use triangle similarity to show that ABCD ~ WXYZ.

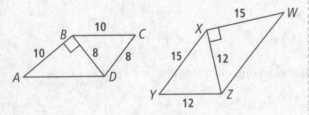

Do You KNOW HOW?

For Exercises 5 and 6, explain whether the two triangles are similar.

5.
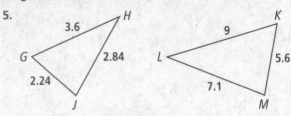

6.
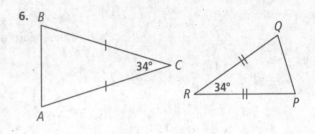

For Exercises 7 and 8, find the value of each variable such that the triangles are similar.

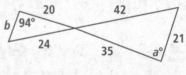

7. a

8. b

9. When Esteban looks at the puddle, he sees a reflection of the top of a cactus. How tall is the cactus?

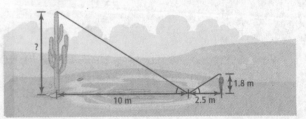

EXPLORE & REASON

Suppose you cut a rectangular piece of paper to create three right triangles.

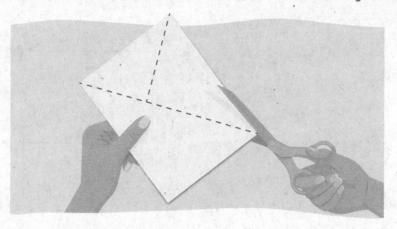

A. Use Appropriate Tools How can you compare leg lengths and angle measures among the triangles? ⓒ **MP.5**

B. Are any of the triangles similar to each other? Explain.

HABITS OF MIND

Generalize How would you use the rectangle to predict side length ratios of triangles created in this way? ⓒ **MP.8**

EXAMPLE 1

Try It! Identify Similar Triangles Formed by an Altitude

1. How is △ACD related to △CBD? Explain.

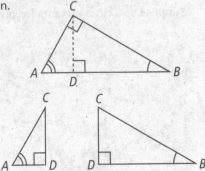

EXAMPLE 2

Try It! Find Missing Lengths Within Right Triangles

2. Refer to △PQR.

a. Write a proportion that you can use to solve for *PS*.

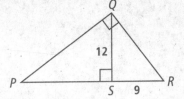

b. What is *PS*?

HABITS OF MIND

Make Sense and Persevere What strategy can you apply to be sure you are comparing corresponding sides of two similar triangles? © MP.1

EXAMPLE 3

Try It! Relate Altitude and Geometric Mean

3. Use △ABC.

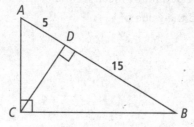

a. What is CD?

b. Describe how you can use the value you found for CD to find AC and CB.

EXAMPLE 4

Try It! Relate Side Lengths and Geometric Mean

4. Use △JKL.

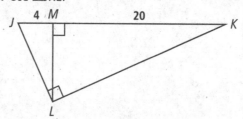

a. What is JL?

b. What is KL?

EXAMPLE 5

Try It! Use the Geometric Mean to Solve Problems

5. Use the geometric mean to find each unknown.

a. Find the value of y.

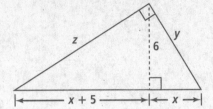

b. Find the value of z.

HABITS OF MIND

Communicate Precisely Corollary 2 to Theorem 7-4 states "The altitude to the hypotenuse of a right triangle divides the hypotenuse so that the length of a given leg is the geometric mean of the length of the hypotenuse and the length of the segment of hypotenuse that is adjacent to the leg." How could you state this in your own words? © MP.6

EXAMPLE 6

Try It! Apply Geometric Mean to Find a Distance

6. Zhang constructs a 4-ft high loading ramp. The length of the back of the base is 12.8 ft and the entire base is 14.05 feet. How long should Zhang make the ramp?

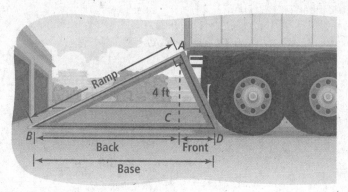

HABITS OF MIND

Construct Arguments How do you know which theorem or corollary to apply on right triangles with an altitude to the hypotenuse? ⓒ MP.3

Do You UNDERSTAND?

1. **ESSENTIAL QUESTION** In a right triangle, what is the relationship between the altitude to the hypotenuse, triangle similarity, and the geometric mean?

2. **Error Analysis** Chris is asked to find a geometric mean in $\triangle JKL$. What is his error? © **MP.3**

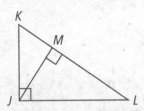

$$\triangle JKL \sim \triangle MKJ$$

$$\frac{KL}{JK} = \frac{JK}{JM}$$ ✗

3. **Vocabulary** Do the altitudes to the legs of a right triangle also create similar triangles? Explain.

Do You KNOW HOW?

For Exercises 4–6, use $\triangle DEF$ to find the lengths.

4. *ER*

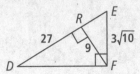

5. *DF*

6. *DE*

For Exercises 7–9, use $\triangle PQR$ to find the lengths.

7. *QA*

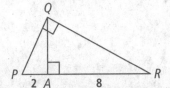

8. *PQ*

9. *QR*

10. Deshawn installs a shelf bracket. What is the widest shelf that will fit without overhang? Explain.

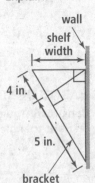

Make It Right

Architects often make a scale physical model of a new building project. The scale model is usually a miniature version of the project it is representing.

When making a model, architects need to make sure that all of the parts of the model are the right size. Think about this during the Mathematical Modeling in 3 Acts lesson.

ACT 1 ▶ Identify the Problem

1. What is the first question that comes to mind after watching the video?

2. Write down the Main Question you will answer about what you saw in the video.

3. Make an initial conjecture that answers this main question.

4. Explain how you arrived at your conjecture.

5. What information will be useful to know to answer the main question? How can you get it? How will you use that information?

ACT 2 Develop a Model

6. Use the math that you have learned in the topic to refine your conjecture.

ACT 3 Interpret the Results

7. Did your refined conjecture match the actual answer exactly? If not, what might explain the difference?

EXPLORE & REASON

Draw a triangle, like the one shown, by dividing one side into four congruent
segments and drawing lines parallel to one of the other sides.

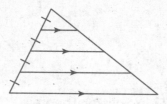

A. How many similar triangles are in the figure? Explain.

B. Look for Relationships How are the lengths of the parallel segments related
to each other? ⒸMP.7

HABITS OF MIND

Look for Relationships How can you find the relationship of the sides of the
similar triangles without any values given? ⒸMP.7

LESSON 7-5 Proportions in Triangles   183

EXAMPLE 1

Try It! Explore Proportions from Parallel Lines

1. $\overline{BD}$ bisects sides $\overline{AC}$ and $\overline{CE}$. Is $\overline{AE} \parallel \overline{BD}$? Explain.

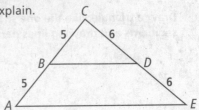

EXAMPLE 2

Try It! Use the Side-Splitter Theorem

2. Refer to $\triangle PQR$.

   a. What is the value of y? Explain.

   b. What is the value of z? Explain.

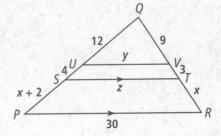

EXAMPLE 3

Try It! Find a Length

3. In the figure of the window, the length of side a is 9.6 ft, side x is 11ft, and side y is 4.4 ft. Apply the Side-Splitter Theorem to find the lengths of b and c. Round your answers to the nearest tenth of a foot.

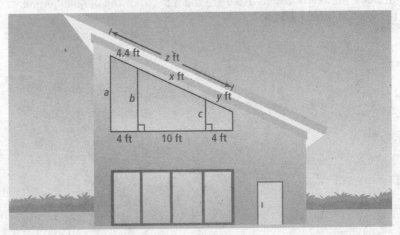

- -

HABITS OF MIND

Use Structure How can you describe the relationship between the Side-Splitter Theorem and the Triangle Midsegment Theorem? © MP.7

EXAMPLE 4

Try It! Investigate Proportionality with an Angle Bisector.

4. Draw $\overrightarrow{ML}$ and a line through K parallel to $\overline{NL}$. Let P be the point of intersection.

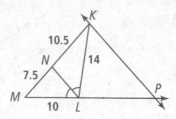

a. Is △MNL ~ △MKP? Explain.

b. Is ∠LKP ≅ ∠LPK? Explain.

EXAMPLE 5

Try It! Use the Triangle-Angle-Bisector Theorem

5. a. What is the value of x?

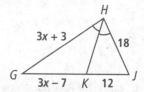

b. What are the values of GH and GK?

HABITS OF MIND

Make Sense and Persevere What information do you need in order to apply the Triangle-Angle Bisector Theorem? ⓒ **MP.1**

Do You UNDERSTAND?

1. **ESSENTIAL QUESTION** When parallel lines intersect two transversals, what are the relationships among the lengths of the segments formed?

2. **Error Analysis** Carmen thinks that $AD = BD$. What is Carmen's error? © MP.3

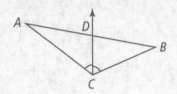

3. **Make Sense and Persevere** What information is needed to determine if x is half of y? © MP.1

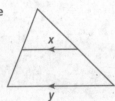

4. **Look for Relationships** If $\overline{RS} \cong \overline{QS}$, what type of triangle is $\triangle PQR$? Use the Triangle-Angle-Bisector Theorem to explain your reasoning. © MP.7

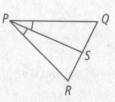

5. **Construct Arguments** Explain why LP must be less than LM. © MP.3

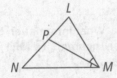

Do You KNOW HOW?

For Exercises 6–11, find each value of x.

6.

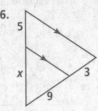

7.

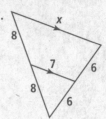

8.

9.

10.

11.

TOPIC 7 Similarity

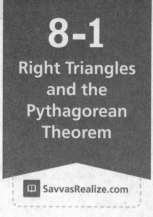
Consider △ABC with altitude $\overline{CD}$ as shown.

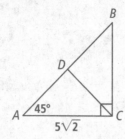

A. What is the area of △ABC? Of △ACD? Explain your answers.

B. Find the lengths of $\overline{AD}$ and $\overline{AB}$.

C. Look for Relationships Divide the length of the hypotenuse of △ABC by the length of one of its sides. Divide the length of the hypotenuse of △ACD by the length of one of its sides. Make a conjecture that explains the results. ⓒ MP.7

HABITS OF MIND

Construct Arguments Do you think that the ratio of the hypotenuse to a leg is the same for all isosceles right triangles? Explain. ⓒ MP.3

EXAMPLE 1

Try It! Use Similarity to Prove the Pythagorean Theorem

1. Find the unknown side length of each right triangle.

a. *AB*

b. *EF*

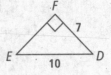

EXAMPLE 2

Try It! Use the Pythagorean Theorem and Its Converse

2. a. What is *KL*?

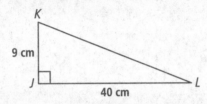

b. Is △*MNO* a right triangle? Explain.

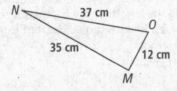

- -

HABITS OF MIND

Communicate Precisely What do you need to know about a figure to apply the Pythagorean Theorem? ⓒ **MP.6**

EXAMPLE 3

Try It! Investigate Side Lengths in 45°-45°-90° Triangles

3. Find the side lengths of each 45°-45°-90° triangle.

   a. What are *XZ* and *YZ*?   b. What are *JK* and *LK*?

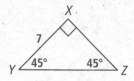
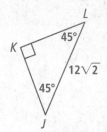

EXAMPLE 4

Try It! Explore the Side Lengths of a 30°-60°-90° Triangle

4. a. What are *PQ* and *PR*?   b. What are *UV* and *TV*?

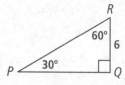
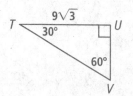

EXAMPLE 5

Try It! Apply Special Right Triangle Relationships

5. a. What are *AB* and *BC*?   b. What are *AC* and *BC*?

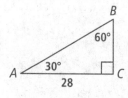
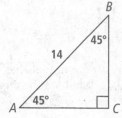

- -

HABITS OF MIND

Model With Mathematics How would you find the height of an equilateral triangle with side *s*? © MP.4

Do You UNDERSTAND?

1. **ESSENTIAL QUESTION** How are similarity in right triangles and the Pythagorean Theorem related?

2. **Error Analysis** Casey was asked to find XY. What is Casey's error? **© MP.3**

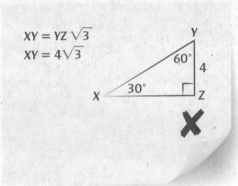

$XY = YZ \sqrt{3}$
$XY = 4\sqrt{3}$

3. **Reason** A right triangle has leg lengths 4.5 and $4.5\sqrt{3}$. What are the measures of the angles? Explain. **© MP.2**

Do You KNOW HOW?

For Exercises 4 and 5, find the value of *x*.

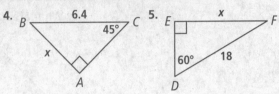

For Exercises 6–8, is △RST a right triangle? Explain.

6. $RS = 20$, $ST = 21$, $RT = 29$

7. $RS = 35$, $ST = 36$, $RT = 71$

8. $RS = 40$, $ST = 41$, $RT = 11$

9. Zaid wants to hang the pennant shown vertically between two windows that are 19 inches apart. Will the pennant fit? Explain.

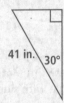

41 in.   30°

CRITIQUE & EXPLAIN

A teacher asked students to write a proportion using the lengths of the legs of the two right triangles.

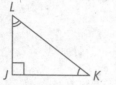

Two students' responses are shown.

Diego

$$\frac{JK}{MN} = \frac{JL}{MO}$$

Rebecca

$$\frac{JK}{JL} = \frac{MN}{MO}$$

A. Do you think that the proportion that Diego wrote is correct? Explain.

B. Do you think that the proportion that Rebecca wrote is correct? Explain.

C. Use Structure If $\frac{a}{b} = \frac{c}{d}$, how can you get an equivalent equation such that the left side of the equation is $\frac{a}{c}$? © MP.7

HABITS OF MIND

Communicate Precisely How can you write a proportion that uses the hypotenuses of two similar triangles? Explain. © MP.6

EXAMPLE 1

Try It! Understand Trigonometric Ratios Using Similarity

1. Show that any two acute angles with the same measure have the same cosine.

EXAMPLE 2

Try It! Write Trigonometric Ratios

2. What are the sine, cosine, and tangent ratios of ∠F?

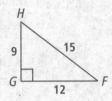

EXAMPLE 3

Try It! Trigonometric Ratios of Special Angles

3. **a.** In △FGH, what is the value of y?

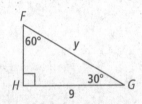

b. How can you write an equivalent expression for cos 70° using sine? An equivalent expression for sin 34° using cosine?

c. Given sin 65° ≈ 0.91, what is the approximate value of cos 25°?

HABITS OF MIND

Generalize How do you know whether to use a trigonometric ratio to solve a problem? ⓒ MP.8

EXAMPLE 4

Try It! Use Trigonometric Ratios to Find Distances

4. If a plane climbs at 5° and flies 20 miles through the air as it climbs, what is the altitude of the airplane, to the nearest foot?

EXAMPLE 5

Try It! Use Trigonometric Inverses to Find Angle Measures

5.

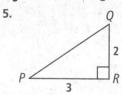

a. What is $m\angle P$?

b. What is $m\angle Q$?

HABITS OF MIND

Use Appropriate Tools Suppose $\tan x° = k$. What expression or series of keystrokes can you use to find the value of x? Ⓒ **MP.5**

Do You UNDERSTAND?

1. **ESSENTIAL QUESTION** How do trigonometric ratios relate angle measures to side lengths of right triangles?

2. **Error Analysis** What is the error in this equation for a trigonometric ratio? © MP.3

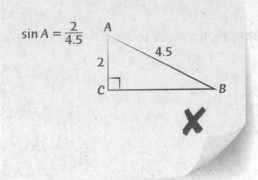

$$\sin A = \frac{2}{4.5}$$

3. **Vocabulary** How are finding the inverses of trigonometric ratios similar to using inverse operations?

4. **Communicate Precisely** How is the sine ratio similar to the cosine ratio? How is it different? © MP.6

5. **Look for Relationships** If $\sin A = \frac{a}{c}$, how could you use a and c to find $\cos A$? © MP.7

6. **Reason** What is an expression for d using $x°$, $y°$, and h? © MP.2

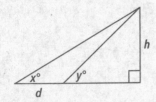

Do You KNOW HOW?

For Exercises 7–12, use $\triangle ABC$ to find each trigonometric ratio or angle measure.

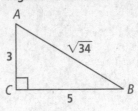

7. tan B

8. cos B

9. sin A

10. tan A

11. $m\angle B$

12. $m\angle A$

13. What are the sine and cosine of the smallest angle in the right triangle shown?

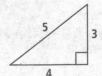

14. What is the measure of the largest acute angle in the right triangle shown?

15. In the figure shown, what are $m\angle S$ and $m\angle T$?

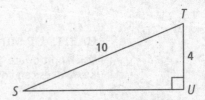

EXPLORE & REASON

Consider the 30°-60°-90° triangle shown.

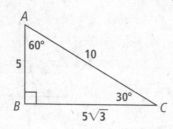

A. Calculate the values of the ratios $\frac{\sin A}{BC}$ and $\frac{\sin C}{AB}$. How are the values of the ratios related?

B. Make Sense and Persevere Do you think the ratios would have the same relationship in any 30°-60°-90° right triangle? Explain your answer. ©️ **MP.1**

HABITS OF MIND

Look for Relationships What general patterns or relationships seem to occur in a triangle between each angle and its opposite side? ©️ **MP.7**

EXAMPLE 1

Try It! Explore the Sine Ratio

1. Show that $\frac{\sin A}{a} = \frac{\sin B}{b} = \frac{\sin C}{c}$.

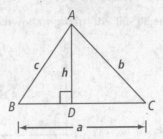

EXAMPLE 2

Try It! Use the Law of Sines to find a Side Length

2. What is *XZ* to the nearest tenth?

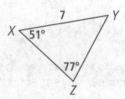

HABITS OF MIND

Reason How can you use the Law of Sines if given the measures of two angles and a side, but not a side opposite either of the two given angles? © **MP.2**

EXAMPLE 3

Try It! Use Law of Sines to Find the Measure of an Angle

3.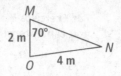

   a. What is $m\angle N$?   **b.** What is $m\angle O$?

EXAMPLE 4

Try It! Apply the Law of Sines

4. Suppose a pilot chose to fly north of a storm between Omaha and Chicago. How much farther is that route than the direct route?

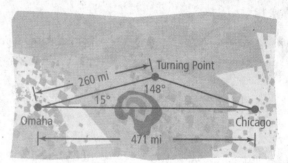

HABITS OF MIND

Communicate Precisely What information do you need to use the Law of Sines to solve a problem? © MP.6

Do You UNDERSTAND?

1. **ESSENTIAL QUESTION** How can the Law of Sines be used to determine side lengths and angle measures in acute and obtuse triangles?

2. **Error Analysis** Amelia is asked to find a missing side length in △RST. What is her error? ⒸMP.3

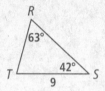

$$\frac{\sin R}{RT} = \frac{\sin S}{ST}$$

$$\frac{\sin 63°}{RT} = \frac{\sin 42°}{9}$$

$$RT = \frac{9 \sin 63°}{\sin 42°} \approx 12$$

✗

3. **Vocabulary** What are the pairs of opposite angles and side lengths in △LMN? What does the Law of Sines help you find?

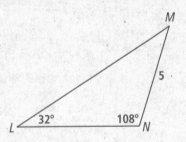

4. **Reason** Can you find all the missing parts of a triangle using the Law of Sines if you know the lengths of all three sides? Explain. ⒸMP.2

Do You KNOW HOW?

For Exercises 5 and 6, list the parts of each triangle you can determine using the Law of Sines.

5.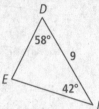

6.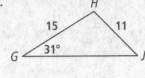

For Exercises 7 and 8, use △QRS.

7. What are m∠Q and m∠R?

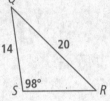

8. What is the perimeter of △QRS?

For Exercises 9 and 10, use △XYZ.

9. What is XY?

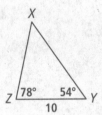

10. What is XZ?

11. What are AB and BC?

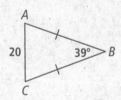

12. What is the perimeter of △TUV?

EXPLORE & REASON

Use △ABC to answer the questions.

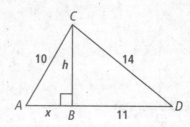

A. Write equations for the side lengths of △ABC and △CBD using the Pythagorean Theorem.

B. Use a system of equations to solve for x.

C. Use Structure How can you use the information you found to determine $m\angle A$? © MP.7

HABITS OF MIND

Look for Relationships Does constructing an altitude in a triangle always divide a triangle into similar triangles? Explain. © MP.7

EXAMPLE 1

Try It! Develop the Law of Cosines with Trigonometry

1. Write equations for a^2 using cos A and b^2 using cos B.

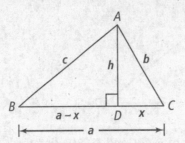

EXAMPLE 2

Try It! Use the Law of Cosines to Find a Side Length

2. a. What is DE?   b. What is GH?

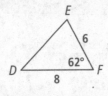
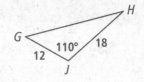

HABITS OF MIND

Construct Arguments Once you use the cosine to find the length of the third side of a triangle, is it possible to find the measures of the other two angles? Explain. © **MP.3**

EXAMPLE 3

Try It! Use the Law of Cosines to Find an Angle Measure

3. a. What is $m\angle X$?

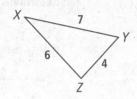

b. What is $m\angle P$?

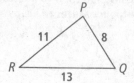

EXAMPLE 4

Try It! Use the Law of Cosines to Solve a Problem

4. The distance from Bald Mountain to the Fire Tower is 1.6 mi. What is the measure of the angle formed by the path from Bald Mountain to the Ranger Station and the path from Bald Mountain to the Fire Tower?

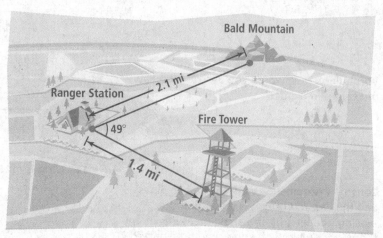

HABITS OF MIND

Make Sense and Persevere. How can you determine whether the Law of Cosines can be used to solve a real-world problem? Ⓒ MP.1

Do You UNDERSTAND?

1. **ESSENTIAL QUESTION** How can the Law of Cosines be used to determine side lengths and angle measures of acute and obtuse triangles?

2. **Error Analysis** Cameron is asked to find *DE*. What is his error? © MP.3

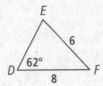

$$DE^2 = DF^2 + EF^2 - 2(DF)(EF)\cos F$$
$$DE^2 = 8^2 + 6^2 - 2(8)(6)\cos 62°$$
$$DE^2 = 54.930\ldots$$
$$DE = 7.411\ldots$$ ✗

3. **Vocabulary** How would you describe the Law of Cosines in words?

4. **Construct Arguments** With the Law of Sines and the Law of Cosines, can you find the missing side lengths and angle measures of any triangle for which you know any three parts? Explain. © MP.3

5. **Reason** Use the Law of Cosines and the Pythagorean Theorem with △*ABC* to show that cos 90° = 0. © MP.2

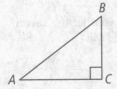

Do You KNOW HOW?

For Exercises 6–9, list the parts of each triangle you can determine using the Law of Cosines.

6.

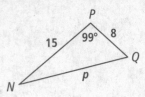

7.

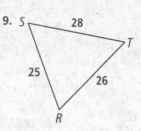

8.

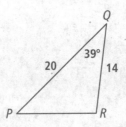

9.

10. What is *PR* to the nearest tenth?

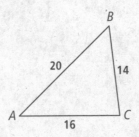

11. What is *m∠B* to the nearest tenth of a degree?

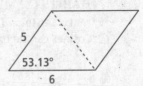

12. Use the Law of Cosines to find the diagonal of the parallelogram.

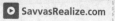

MATHEMATICAL
MODELING
IN **3** ACTS

 SavvasRealize.com

The Impossible Measurement

Tall buildings are often some of the most recognizable structures of cities. The Empire State Building in New York City, the Transamerica Pyramid in San Francisco, and the JPMorgan Chase Tower in Houston are all famous landmarks in those cities.

Cities around the world compete for the tallest building bragging rights. Which city currently has the tallest building? This Mathematical Modeling in 3 Acts lesson will get you thinking about the height of structures, including tall buildings such as these.

ACT 1 Identify the Problem

1. What is the first question that comes to mind after watching the video?

2. Write down the main question you will answer about what you saw in the video.

3. Make an initial conjecture that answers this main question.

4. Explain how you arrived at your conjecture.

5. What information will be useful to know to answer the main question? How can you get it? How will you use that information?

ACT 2 ▸ Develop a Model

6. Use the math that you have learned in the topic to refine your conjecture.

ACT 3 ▸ Interpret the Results

7. Did your refined conjecture match the actual answer exactly? If not, what might explain the difference?

MODEL & DISCUSS

A search-and-rescue team is having a nighttime practice drill. Two members of the team are in a helicopter that is hovering at 2,000 feet above ground level.

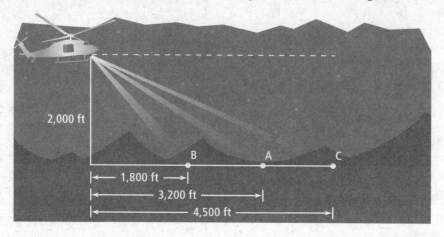

A. The team first tries to locate object A. At what angle from the horizontal line even with the helicopter should they position the spotlight so that it shines on object A?

B. Next, they shine the spotlight on object B. How does the angle of the spotlight from the horizontal line change?

C. Use Structure In general, how does the angle of the spotlight from the horizontal change as the light moves from object A to object B? From object A to object C? © MP.7

HABITS OF MIND

Use Appropriate Tools What geometric figures are useful in modeling situations where you want to find angle measures? Why are these figures helpful? © MP.7

EXAMPLE 1

Try It! Identify Angles of Elevation and Depression

1. How does the angle of depression, ∠1, compare with the angle of elevation, ∠2? Explain your reasoning.

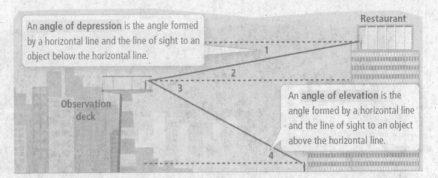

An **angle of depression** is the angle formed by a horizontal line and the line of sight to an object below the horizontal line.

An **angle of elevation** is the angle formed by a horizontal line and the line of sight to an object above the horizontal line.

Restaurant

Observation deck

EXAMPLE 2

Try It! Use Angles of Elevation and Depression

2. Nadeem is standing 180 feet above the ground on top of a tower. He looks down at a tour bus at an angle of depression of 23°. To the nearest foot, how far is the bus from the base of the tower?

HABITS OF MIND

Communicate Precisely How can you relate angles of elevation and depression to parallel lines intersected by a transversal? © MP.6

EXAMPLE 3

Try It! Use Trigonometry to Solve Problems

3. An instructor holds a safety rope at point *C* for a student to repel 16 ft from point *T* to a resting point at *R*. How far is the student from the instructor at the resting point?

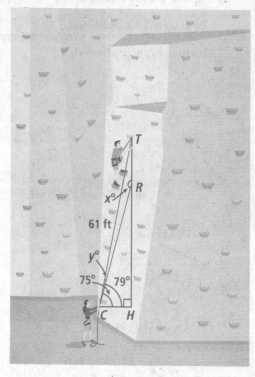

EXAMPLE 4

Try It! Use Trigonometry to Find Triangle Area

4. a. What is the area of △*JKL*?

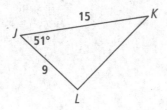

b. What is the area of △*PQR*?

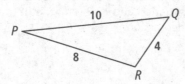

HABITS OF MIND

Reason What quantities do you need to know if you want to apply the Law of Sines or Cosines to solve a problem? Ⓒ **MP.2**

Do You UNDERSTAND?

1. **ESSENTIAL QUESTION** How can trigonometry be used to solve real-world and mathematical problems?

2. **Error Analysis** What error does Rashon make in finding the area? **© MP.3**

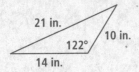

21 in.
10 in.
122°
14 in.

$A = \frac{1}{2} bc \sin A$

$A = \frac{1}{2} \cdot 210 \cdot 0.8480$

Area is about 89 in.^{2}

✗

3. **Vocabulary** A person on a balcony and a person on a street are looking at each other. Draw a diagram to represent the situation and label the angles of elevation and depression.

4. **Make Sense and Persevere** How do you find the area of a triangle when given only the lengths of three sides? **© MP.1**

Do You KNOW HOW?

5. A person rides a glass elevator in a hotel lobby. As the elevator goes up, how does the angle of depression to a fixed point on the lobby floor change?

6. A person observes the top of a radio antenna at an angle of elevation of 5°. After getting 1 mile closer to the antenna, the angle of elevation is 10°. How tall is the antenna to the nearest tenth of a foot?

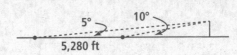

5°   10°

5,280 ft

7. Triangle ABC has AB = 13, AC = 15, and m∠A = 59. What is the area of the triangle to the nearest tenth?

8. Triangle DEF has DE = 13, DF = 15, and EF = 14. What is the area of the triangle to the nearest tenth?

9. A temporary pen for cattle is built using 10-foot sections of fence arranged in a triangle. One side of the pen has 4 sections, one has 5 sections, and the last has 6 sections. What is the area enclosed by the pen?

EXPLORE & REASON

Players place game pieces
on the board shown and
earn points from the
attributes of the piece
placed on the board.

- 1 point for a right angle
- 2 points for a pair of
  parallel sides
- 3 points for the shortest
  perimeter

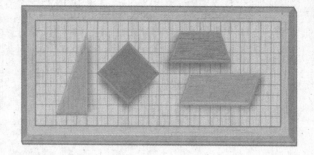

A. Which game piece is worth the greatest total points? Explain.

B. **Make Sense and Persevere** Describe a way to determine the perimeters
that is different from the way you chose. Which method do you consider
better? Explain. © MP.1

HABITS OF MIND

Communicate Precisely How can you compare the lengths of sides of polygons
that are placed on grids? © MP.6

EXAMPLE 1

Try It! Connect Algebra and Geometry Through Coordinates

1. Given △ABC, what is the length of the line segment connecting the midpoints of $\overline{AC}$ and $\overline{BC}$?

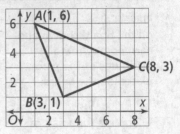

EXAMPLE 2

Try It! Classify a Triangle on the Coordinate Plane

2. The vertices of △PQR are P(4, 1), Q(2, 7), and R(8, 5).

  a. Is △PQR equilateral, isosceles, or scalene? Explain.

  b. Is △PQR a right triangle? Explain.

HABITS OF MIND

Look for Relationships Given the vertices of a triangle on a coordinate plane, what formulas can you use to determine the type of triangle? Explain. © MP.7

EXAMPLE 3

Try It! Classify a Parallelogram on the Coordinate Plane

3. The vertices of a parallelogram are $A(-2, 2)$, $B(4, 6)$, $C(6, 3)$, and $D(0, -1)$.

    a. Is $ABCD$ a rhombus? Explain.   b. Is $ABCD$ a rectangle? Explain.

EXAMPLE 4

Try It! Classify Quadrilaterals as Trapezoids and Kites on the Coordinate Plane

4. Is each quadrilateral a kite, trapezoid, or neither?

  a.

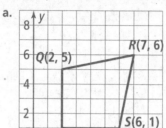

  b.

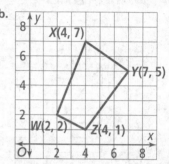

EXAMPLE 5

Try It! Find Perimeter and Area

5. The vertices of $WXYZ$ are $W(5, 4)$, $X(2, 9)$, $Y(9, 9)$, and $Z(8, 4)$.

    a. What is the perimeter of $WXYZ$?   b. What is the area of $WXYZ$?

HABITS OF MIND

Use Structure Can the slopes of three of the four sides of a quadrilateral be equal? Explain. © MP.7

Do You UNDERSTAND?

1. **ESSENTIAL QUESTION** How are properties of geometric figures represented in the coordinate plane?

2. **Error Analysis** Chen is asked to describe two methods to find BC. Why is Chen incorrect? © MP.3

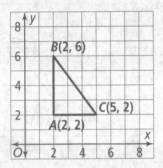

The only possible method is to use the Distance Formula because you only know the endpoints of $\overline{BC}$.

3. **Communicate Precisely** Describe three ways you can determine whether a quadrilateral is a parallelogram given the coordinates of the vertices. © MP.6

Do You KNOW HOW?

Use JKLM for Exercises 4–6.

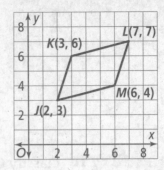

4. What is the perimeter of JKLM?

5. What is the relationship between $\overline{JL}$ and $\overline{KM}$? Explain.

6. What type of quadrilateral is JKLM? Explain.

Use △PQR for Exercises 7 and 8.

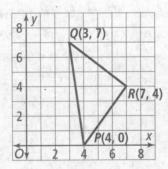

7. What kind of triangle is PQR? Explain.

8. What is the area of PQR?

You Be the Judge

Have you ever been a judge in a contest or competition? What criteria did you use to decide the winner? If you were one of many judges, did you all agree on who should win?

Often there is a set of criteria that judges use to help them score the performances of the contestants. Having criteria helps all of the judges be consistent regardless of the person they are rating. Think of this during the Mathematical Modeling in 3 Acts lesson.

MATHEMATICAL MODELING IN 3 ACTS

ACT 1 ▶ **Identify the Problem**

1. What is the first question that comes to mind after watching the video?

2. Write down the main question you will answer about what you saw in the video.

3. Make an initial conjecture that answers this main question.

4. Explain how you arrived at your conjecture.

5. What information will be useful to know to answer the main question? How can you get it? How will you use that information?

ACT 2 ▶ Develop a Model

6. Use the math that you have learned in this Topic to refine your conjecture.

ACT 3 ▶ Interpret the Results

7. Did your refined conjecture match the actual answer exactly? If not, what might explain the difference?

CRITIQUE & EXPLAIN

Dakota and Jung are trying to show that $\triangle ABC$ is a right triangle. Each student uses a different method.

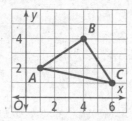

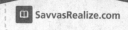
Dakota

slope of $\overline{AB} = \frac{2}{3}$, slope of $\overline{BC} = -\frac{3}{2}$

slope of $\overline{AB} \cdot$ slope of $\overline{BC} = -1$

Triangle ABC is a right triangle.

Jung

$AB = BC = \sqrt{13}$, $AC = \sqrt{26}$

$(\sqrt{13})^2 + (\sqrt{13})^2 = (\sqrt{26})^2$

Triangle ABC is a right triangle.

A. Did Dakota and Jung both show $\triangle ABC$ is a right triangle? Explain.

B. Reason If the coordinates of $\triangle ABC$ were changed to (2, 3), (5, 5), and (7, 2), how would each student's method change? Explain. © MP.2

HABITS OF MIND

Make Sense and Persevere What information about angles or sides might you use to show that a triangle is not a right triangle? Explain. © MP.1

EXAMPLE 1

Try It! Plan a Coordinate Proof

1. Plan a proof to show that the diagonals of a square are congruent and perpendicular.

EXAMPLE 2

Try It! Write a Coordinate Proof

2. Use coordinate geometry to prove that the diagonals of a rectangle are congruent.

HABITS OF MIND

Use Structure If a figure has a pair of parallel sides, how could that help you in determining coordinates to use for your figure? © MP.7

EXAMPLE 3

Try It! Plan and Write a Coordinate Proof

3. Draw a median from point B to point E that intersects medians $\overline{AD}$ and $\overline{CF}$. Label the point of intersection P. Use the Distance Formula to show that $AP = \frac{2}{3}AD$, $BP = \frac{2}{3}BE$, and $CP = \frac{2}{3}CF$.

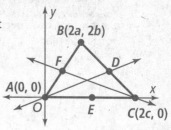

EXAMPLE 4

Try It! Use Coordinate Proofs to Solve Problems

4. A table has a top that is a right triangle and a single support leg. Where should the center of the leg be placed so it corresponds with the center of gravity of the table top? Plan a coordinate geometry proof to find its location.

HABITS OF MIND

Construct Arguments Why might you decide to have one vertex of a figure at the origin? Why might you decide not to? ⓒ MP.3

Do You UNDERSTAND?

1. **ESSENTIAL QUESTION** How can geometric relationships be proven algebraically in the coordinate plane?

2. **Error Analysis** Venetta tried to find the slope of $\overline{AB}$. What is her error? © MP.3

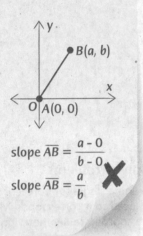

$$\text{slope } \overline{AB} = \frac{a - 0}{b - 0}$$

$$\text{slope } \overline{AB} = \frac{a}{b}$$

3. **Communicate Precisely** What is a coordinate geometry proof? © MP.6

4. **Reason** Describe why it is important to plan a coordinate proof. © MP.2

5. **Use Structure** What coordinates would you use to describe an isosceles triangle on a coordinate plane? Explain. © MP.7

Do You KNOW HOW?

For Exercises 6–8, write a plan for a coordinate proof.

6. The diagonals of a rhombus are perpendicular.

7. The area of a triangle with vertices $A(0, 0)$, $B(0, a)$ and $C(b, c)$ is $\frac{ab}{2}$.

8. The lines that contain the altitudes of a triangle are concurrent.

For Exercises 9–12, plan and write a coordinate proof.

9. A point on the perpendicular bisector of a segment is equidistant from the endpoints.

10. The diagonals of a kite are perpendicular.

11. All squares are similar.

12. The area of a rhombus is half the product of the lengths of its diagonals.

MODEL & DISCUSS

Damian uses an app to find all pizza restaurants within a certain distance of his current location.

A. What is the shape of the region that the app uses to search for pizza restaurants? Explain how you know.

B. What information do you think the app needs to determine the area to search?

C. Construct Arguments If Damian's friend is using the same app from a different location, could the app find the same pizza restaurant for both boys? Explain. © MP.3

HABITS OF MIND

Use Appropriate Tools What geometric figure could you use with a paper map to locate points within a given distance from a given location? What tool would you use? © MP.5

EXAMPLE 1

Try It! Derive the Equation of a Circle

1. What are the radius and center of the circle with the equation $(x - 2)^2 + (y - 3)^2 = 25$?

EXAMPLE 2

Try It! Write the Equation of a Circle

2. What is the equation for each circle?

a.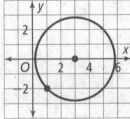

b.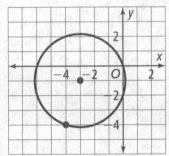

HABITS OF MIND

Use Structure Given the endpoints of the diameter of a circle, how would you find the equation of the circle? © MP.7

EXAMPLE 3

Try It! Determine Whether a Point Lies on a Circle

3. Determine whether each point lies on the given circle.

   a. $(-3, \sqrt{11})$; circle with center at the origin and radius $2\sqrt{5}$

   b. $(6, 3)$; circle with center at $(2, 4)$ and radius $3\sqrt{3}$

EXAMPLE 4

Try It! Complete the Square to Find the Center and Radius of a Circle

4. What is the graph of each circle?

   a. $x^2 + 4x + y^2 = 21$ b. $x^2 + 2x + y^2 - 4y = -4$

EXAMPLE 5

Try It! Use the Graph and Equation of a Circle to Solve Problems

5. A Doppler radar station in Fairfield covers the cities of Fairfield, Greenville, and Haverford, as shown. The range of a second Doppler station is defined by the equation $(x - 330)^2 + (y - 150)^2 = 8100$. Will the station cover the remaining three cities? Explain.

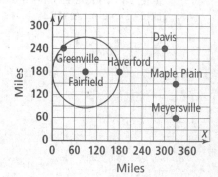

HABITS OF MIND

Use Structure How can you verify that an equation of a circle agrees with the graph of the circle? © MP.7

Do You UNDERSTAND?

1. **ESSENTIAL QUESTION** How is the equation of a circle determined in the coordinate plane?

2. **Error Analysis** Leo says that the equation for the circle is $(x - 1)^2 + (y - 2)^2 = 3$. What is his error? © MP.3

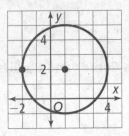

3. **Construct Arguments** If you are given the coordinates of the center and one point on a circle, can you determine the equation of the circle? Explain. © MP.3

4. **Make Sense and Persevere** How could you write the equation of a circle given only the coordinates of the endpoints of its diameter? © MP.1

Do You KNOW HOW?

5. What are the center and radius of the circle with equation $(x - 4)^2 + (y - 9)^2 = 1$?

6. What is the equation for the circle with center (6, 2) and radius 8?

7. What are the center and radius of the circle with equation $(x + 7)^2 + (y - 1)^2 = 9$?

8. What is the equation for the circle with center (−9, 5) and radius 4?

For Exercises 9 and 10, write an equation for each circle shown.

9. 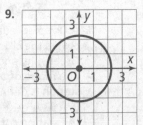   10.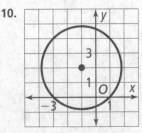

11. Is point (5, −2) on the circle with radius 5 and center (8, 2)?

12. What is the equation for the circle with center (5, 11) that passes through (9, −2)?

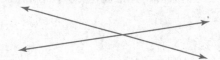
EXPLORE & REASON

Consider two points and two intersecting lines.

A. Describe the set of points that are equidistant from two points. Draw a diagram to support your answer.

B. Describe the set of points that are equidistant from two intersecting lines. Draw a diagram to support your answer.

C. Look for Relationships What do you think a set of points that are equidistant from a line and a point would look like? Draw a diagram to support your answer. ©️ MP.7

HABITS OF MIND

Make Sense and Persevere What is the point or set of points in a plane equidistant from two parallel lines? Explain how you know. ©️ MP.1

EXAMPLE 1

Try It! Explore the Graph of a Parabola

1. The set of points equidistant from (3, 5) and the line $y = 9$ is also a parabola.

   a. What is the vertex of the parabola?

   b. Describe the graph of the parabola.

EXAMPLE 2

Try It! Derive the Equation of a Parabola

2. What expression represents the distance between the focus and the directrix?

HABITS OF MIND

Use Structure How would the parabola be different if the directrix is above the focus on the coordinate plane? © MP.7

EXAMPLE 3

Try It! **Write the Equation of a Parabola**

3. a. What equation represents the parabola with focus (−1, 4) and directrix $y = -2$?

b. What equation represents the parabola with focus (3, 5) and vertex (3, −1)?

EXAMPLE 4

Try It! **Apply the Equation of a Parabola**

4. On a satellite dish, the feed horn is 38 inches above the vertex. If the height of the dish is 22 inches, what is its width?

HABITS OF MIND

Communicate Precisely How can you find the focus of parabola given the vertex and the directrix? © **MP.6**

Do You UNDERSTAND?

1. **ESSENTIAL QUESTION** How does the geometric description of a parabola relate to its equation?

2. **Error Analysis** Arthur says that an equation of the parabola with directrix $y = 0$ and focus $= (0, 6)$ is $y - 3 = \frac{1}{24}x^2$. What is his error? © **MP.3**

3. **Vocabulary** How could the word *direction* help you remember that the directrix is a line?

4. **Reason** What are the coordinates of point P? Show your work. © **MP.2**

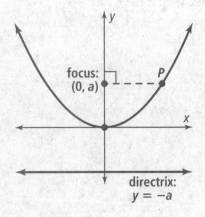

5. **Communicate Precisely** Given vertex (a, b) and focus (a, c), describe how you would write an equation for the parabola. © **MP.6**

Do You KNOW HOW?

For Exercises 6 and 7, write an equation of each parabola with the given focus and directrix.

6. focus: $(5, 1)$; directrix: $y = -5$

7. focus: $(0, 4)$; directrix: $y = -4$

For Exercises 8 and 9, give the vertex, focus, and directrix of each parabola.

8. $y - 2 = \frac{1}{6}x^2$

9. $y + 3 = \frac{1}{20}(x - 9)^2$

For Exercises 10 and 11, write an equation of each parabola with the given focus and vertex.

10. focus: $(6, 2)$; vertex: $(6, -4)$

11. focus: $(-1, 8)$; vertex: $(-1, 7)$

12. What is the equation of the parabola graphed on the coordinate plane?

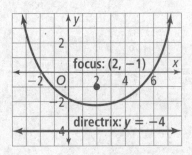

13. Consider the parabola $y = \frac{1}{36}x^2$.

    a. What are the focus and directrix?

    b. The parabola passes through $(12, 4)$. Show that this point is equidistant from the focus and the directrix.

EXPLORE & REASON

Darren bends a piece of wire using a circular disc to make the shape as shown.

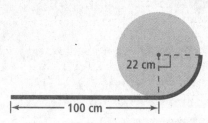

22 cm

←——— 100 cm ———→

A. How long does the piece of wire need to be to make the shape? Explain.

B. Construct Arguments What information do you think is needed to find part of the circumference of a circle? Justify your answer. © **MP.3**

HABITS OF MIND

Model With Mathematics Write an expression that represents the circular part of the wire. Explain what each part of your expression represents. © **MP.4**

EXAMPLE 1

Try It! Relate Central Angles and Arc Measures

1. Use ⊙W.
   a. What is m$\overset{\frown}{XZ}$?

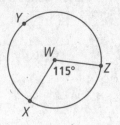

   b. What is m$\overset{\frown}{XYZ}$?

EXAMPLE 2

Try It! Relate Arc Length to Circumference

2. The two circles share center O. The larger circle is a dilation of the smaller circle with scale factor 1.5. The measure of ∠AOB is 60° and the measure of arc CD is 2π.

   a. What is the length of arc AB? Round to the nearest tenth.

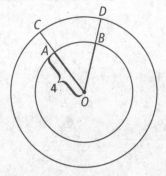

   b. Show that the measures of ∠AOB and ∠COD, in radians, are equal.

EXAMPLE 3

Try It! Apply Arc Length

3. Use ⊙Q. Express answers in terms of π.

a. What is the length of $\overarc{JK}$?

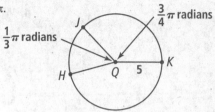

b. What is the length of $\overarc{HK}$?

HABITS OF MIND

Reason How would you describe the relationships between arc length, arc measure, and circumference? ⒸMP.2

EXAMPLE 4

Try It! Relate the Area of a Circle to the Area of a Sector

4. What is the area of each shaded sector?

a.

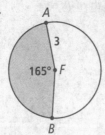

b.

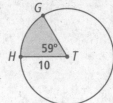

EXAMPLE 5

Try It! Find the Area of a Segment of a Circle

5. What is the area of each segment?

a.

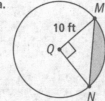

b.

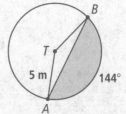

EXAMPLE 6

Try It! Solve Problems Involving Circles

6. What are the area and perimeter of sector *QNR*? Round to the nearest tenth.

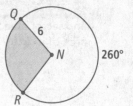

HABITS OF MIND

Generalize Is it always true that the area of a segment is less than the area of the corresponding sector? Explain. © MP.8

Do You UNDERSTAND?

1. **ESSENTIAL QUESTION** How are arc length and sector area related to circumference and area of a circle?

2. **Error Analysis** Luke was asked to compute the length of $\overset{\frown}{AB}$. What is Luke's error? © **MP.3**

1.5 radians

$$S = \frac{n}{360} \cdot 2\pi r$$
$$= \frac{1.5}{360} \cdot 2\pi(3)$$
$$= 0.0785 \quad \text{✗}$$

3. **Vocabulary** How can the word *segment* help you remember what a *segment of a circle* is?

4. **Reason** Mercedes says that she can find the area of a quarter of a circle using the formula $A = \frac{1}{4}\pi r^2$. Using the formula for the area of a sector, explain why Mercedes is correct. © **MP.2**

Do You KNOW HOW?

For Exercises 5 and 6, find the measures and lengths of each arc. Express the answers in terms of π.

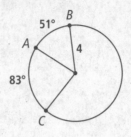

51°   83°   4

5. $\overset{\frown}{BC}$

6. $\overset{\frown}{ABC}$

7. Circle P has radius 8. Points Q and R lie on circle P, and the length of $\overset{\frown}{QR}$ is 4π. What is $m\angle QPR$ in radians?

8. What is the area of sector EFG? Express the answer in terms of π.

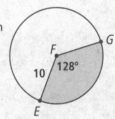

10   128°

9. What is the area of the segment? Express the answer in terms of π.

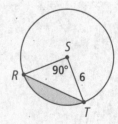

90°   6

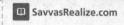
CRITIQUE & EXPLAIN

Alicia and Renaldo made conjectures about the lines that intersect a circle only once.

Alicia

- Many lines intersect the circle once at the same point.
- Two lines that intersect the circle once and the segment connecting the points form an isosceles triangle.

Renaldo

- Parallel lines intersect the circle at opposite ends of the same diameter.
- The lines intersecting the circle at one point are perpendicular to a diameter of the circle.

A. Use Appropriate Tools Which of the four conjectures do you agree with? Which do you disagree with? Draw sketches to support your answers. ⓒ **MP.5**

B. What other conjectures can you make about lines that intersect a circle at one point?

HABITS OF MIND

Communicate Precisely What mathematical terms apply in this situation? ⓒ **MP.6**

EXAMPLE 1

Try It! Understand Tangents to a Circle

1. In the diagram, line *m* is tangent to circle *C* at point *X*. Point *Y* is any other point on *m*, and $\overline{CY}$ passes through circle *C* at *Z*. Because $CY = r + ZY$, $CX < CY$. Since this means $\overline{CX}$ is the shortest segment from *C* to line *m*, then $\overline{CX} \perp m$. Does this support Renaldo's conjecture that parallel lines intersect the circle at opposite ends of the same diameter? Explain.

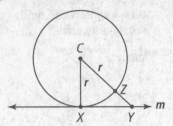

EXAMPLE 2

Try It! Use Tangents to Solve Problems

2. Use ⊙*N*.

a. Is $\overleftrightarrow{MP}$ tangent to ⊙*N*? Explain.

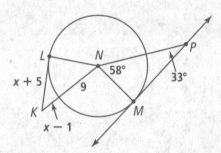

b. If $\overline{LK}$ is tangent to ⊙*N* at *L*, what is *KN*?

- -

HABITS OF MIND

Construct Arguments What are some ways that you can determine whether a line is tangent to a circle? © MP.3

EXAMPLE 3

Try It! Find Lengths of Segments Tangent to a Circle

3. If $TX = 12$ and $TZ = 20$, what are XZ and YZ?

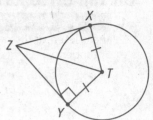

EXAMPLE 4

Try It! Find Measures Involving Tangent Lines

4. What is the perimeter of $ABCD$?

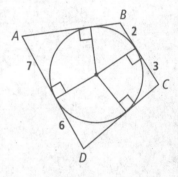

EXAMPLE 5

Try It! Construct Tangent Lines

5. Prove that $\overline{TC}$ is tangent to $\odot P$.

   Given: Concentric circles with center P,
   points A and C on the smaller circle,
   points T and B on the larger circle,
   $\overline{AB} \perp \overline{PT}$

   Prove: $\overline{TC}$ is tangent to $\odot P$ at C.

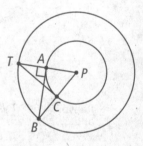

HABITS OF MIND

Generalize Is it always true that there are exactly two tangent lines from a point on the exterior of a circle to the circle? Explain. ⓒ MP.8

Do You UNDERSTAND?

1. **ESSENTIAL QUESTION** How is a tangent line related to the radius of a circle at the point of tangency?

2. **Error Analysis** Kona looked at the figure shown and said that $\overline{AB}$ is tangent to ⊙G at A because it intersects ⊙G only at A. What was Kona's error? ⓒ **MP.3**

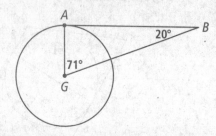

3. **Vocabulary** Can any point on a circle be a *point of tangency*? Explain.

4. **Reason** Lines *m* and *n* are tangent to circles *A* and *B*. What are the relationships between ∠PAS, ∠PQS, ∠RQS, and ∠RBS? Explain. ⓒ **MP.2**

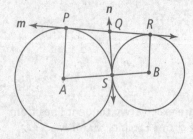

Do You KNOW HOW?

Tell whether each line or segment is a tangent to ⊙B.

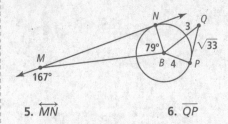

5. $\overleftrightarrow{MN}$

6. $\overline{QP}$

Segment *AC* is tangent to ⊙D at B. Find each value.

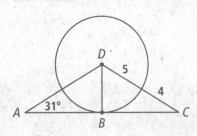

7. m∠ADB

8. *BC*

Segment *FG* is tangent to ⊙K at F and $\overline{HG}$ is tangent to ⊙K at H. Find each value.

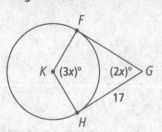

9. *FG*

10. m∠FGH

Earth Watch

Scientists estimate that there are currently about 3,000 operational man-made satellites orbiting Earth. These satellites serve different purposes, from communication to navigation and global positioning. Some are weather satellites that collect environmental information.

The International Space Station is the largest man-made satellite that orbits Earth. It serves as a space environment research facility, and it also offers amazing views of Earth. Think about this during the Mathematical Modeling in 3 Acts lesson.

ACT 1 ▶ Identify the Problem

1. What is the first question that comes to mind after watching the video?

2. Write down the main question you will answer about what you saw in the video.

3. Make an initial conjecture that answers this main question.

4. Explain how you arrived at your conjecture.

5. What information will be useful to know to answer the main question? How can you get it? How will you use that information?

ACT 2 ▸ **Develop a Model**

6. Use the math that you have learned in the Topic to refine your conjecture.

ACT 3 ▸ **Interpret the Results**

7. Did your refined conjecture match the actual answer exactly? If not, what might explain the difference?

EXPLORE & REASON

Use the diagram to answer the questions.

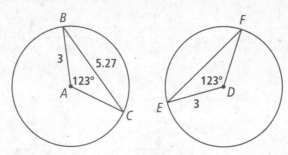

A. What figures in the diagram are congruent? Explain.

B. Look for Relationships How can you find *EF*? © MP.7

HABITS OF MIND

Use Structure What is true of the radii of both circles? Explain. © MP.7

EXAMPLE 1

Try It! Relate Central Angles and Chords

1. Why is ∠BAC ≅ ∠DAE?

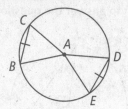

EXAMPLE 2

Try It! Relate Arcs and Chords

2. Write a flow proof of the Converse of Theorem 10-4, which states, "If two chords in a circle or in congruent circles are congruent, then their arcs are congruent."

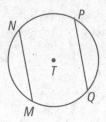

If... $\overline{MN} \cong \overline{PQ}$
Then... $\overarc{MN} \cong \overarc{PQ}$

EXAMPLE 3

Try It! Relate Chords Equidistant from the Center

3. Write a flow proof of the Converse of Theorem 10-5, which states, "If two chords in a circle or in congruent circles are congruent, then they are equidistant from the center or centers."

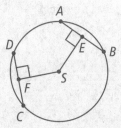

If... $\overline{SE} \cong \overline{SF}$, Then... $\overline{AB} \cong \overline{CD}$
If... $\overline{AB} \cong \overline{CD}$, Then... $\overline{SE} \cong \overline{SF}$

HABITS OF MIND

Generalize In the same circle or in congruent circles, what is true about congruent chords? Ⓒ MP.8

EXAMPLE 4

Try It! Construct a Regular Hexagon Inscribed in a Circle

4. Construct an equilateral triangle inscribed in a circle.

EXAMPLE 5

Try It! Solve Problems Involving Chords of Circles

5. Fresh cut flowers need to be in at least 4 inches of water. A spherical vase is filled until the surface of the water is a circle 5 inches in diameter. Is the water deep enough for the flowers? Explain.

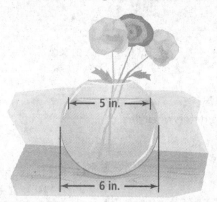

HABITS OF MIND

Reason What is the first thing to look for when solving problems involving chords and diameters? © **MP.2**

Do You UNDERSTAND?

1. **ESSENTIAL QUESTION** How are chords related to their central angles and intercepted arcs?

2. **Error Analysis** Aquene writes a proof to show that two chords are congruent. What is her error? © MP.3

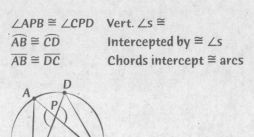

$\angle APB \cong \angle CPD$	Vert. $\angle$s $\cong$
$\overline{AB} \cong \overline{CD}$	Intercepted by $\cong \angle$s
$\overline{AB} \cong \overline{DC}$	Chords intercept $\cong$ arcs

3. **Vocabulary** Explain why all diameters of circles are also chords of the circles.

4. **Reason** Given $\overarc{RS} \cong \overarc{UT}$, how can you find UT? © MP.2

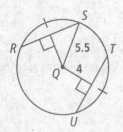

Do You KNOW HOW?

For Exercises 5–10, in $\odot P$, $m\overarc{AB} = 43°$, and $AC = DF$. Find each measure.

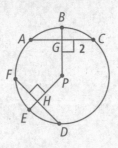

5. DF

6. $m\overarc{AC}$

7. FH

8. $m\overarc{DE}$

9. AC

10. $m\overarc{DF}$

11. For the corporate headquarters, an executive wants to place a company logo that is six feet in diameter with the sides of the H five feet tall on the front wall. What is the width x of the crossbar for the H?

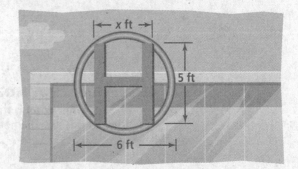

EXPLORE & REASON

Consider ⊙T.

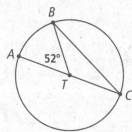

A. **Make Sense and Persevere** List at least seven things you can conclude about the figure. ⓒ MP.1

B. How is ∠ACB related to ∠ATB? Explain.

HABITS OF MIND

Use Structure What is the relationship between a central angle and its intercepted arc? ⓒ MP.7

EXAMPLE 1

Try It! Relate Inscribed Angles to Intercepted Arcs

1. Given $\odot P$ with inscribed angle $\angle S$, if $m\overset{\frown}{RT} = 47$, what is $m\angle S$?

EXAMPLE 2

Try It! Use the Inscribed Angles Theorem

2. a. If $m\overset{\frown}{RST} = 164$, what is $m\angle RVT$?

b. If $m\angle SPU = 79$, what is $m\overset{\frown}{STU}$?

HABITS OF MIND

Communicate Precisely If the center of a circle is in the exterior of an inscribed angle, can the inscribed angle be a right angle? Explain. © MP.6

EXAMPLE 3

Try It! Explore Angles Formed by a Tangent and a Chord

3. a. Given $\overleftrightarrow{BD}$ tangent to ⊙P at point C,
if $m\overset{\frown}{AC} = 88$, what is $m\angle ACB$?

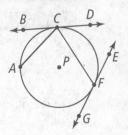

b. Given $\overleftrightarrow{EG}$ tangent to ⊙P at point F, if $m\angle GFC = 115$, what is $m\overset{\frown}{FAC}$?

EXAMPLE 4

Try It! Use Arc Measure to Solve a Problem

4. a. Given $\overleftrightarrow{WY}$ tangent to ⊙C at point X, what is $m\overset{\frown}{XZ}$?

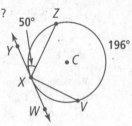

b. What is $m\angle VXW$?

- -

HABITS OF MIND

Reason What can you conclude about the intercepted arc when a tangent and a diameter form an angle? Explain. ⓒ MP.2

Do You UNDERSTAND?

1. **ESSENTIAL QUESTION** How is the measure of an inscribed angle related to its intercepted arc?

2. **Error Analysis** Darren is asked to find $m\widehat{XZ}$. What is his error? © **MP.3**

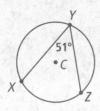

$$mXZ = \frac{1}{2} m\angle XYZ$$
$$= \frac{1}{2}(51)$$
$$= 25.5 \quad \times$$

3. **Reason** Can the measure of an inscribed angle be greater than the measure of the intercepted arc? Explain. © **MP.2**

4. **Make Sense and Persevere** Is there enough information in the diagram to find $m\widehat{RST}$? Explain. © **MP.1**

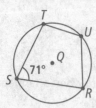

Do You KNOW HOW?

For Exercises 5–8, find each measure in $\odot Q$.

5. $m\widehat{JL}$

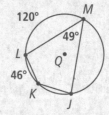

6. $m\widehat{MJ}$

7. $m\angle KJM$

8. $m\angle KLM$

For Exercises 9–12, $\overleftrightarrow{DF}$ is tangent to $\odot O$ at point E. Find each measure.

9. $m\widehat{EH}$

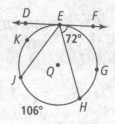

10. $m\widehat{EJ}$

11. $m\angle HEJ$

12. $m\angle DEJ$

For Exercises 13–16, find each measure in $\odot M$.

13. $m\angle PRQ$

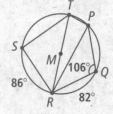

14. $m\angle PTR$

15. $m\angle RST$

16. $m\angle SRT$

EXPLORE & REASON

Skyler made the design shown. Points *A*, *B*, *C*, and *D* are spaced evenly around the circle.

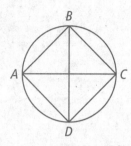

A. Using points *A*, *B*, *C*, and *D* as vertices, what congruent angles can you find? How can you justify that they are congruent?

B. Make Sense and Persevere What strategy did you use to make sure you found all congruent angles? Ⓒ **MP.1**

HABITS OF MIND

Generalize How does the fact that the points are evenly spaced affect your answers? Ⓒ **MP.8**

EXAMPLE 1

Try It! Relate Secants and Angle Measures

1. If $m\widehat{AD} = 155$ and $m\widehat{BC} = 61$, what is $m\angle 1$?

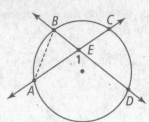

EXAMPLE 2

Try It! Prove Theorem 10-11

2. Theorem 10-11 states, "The measure of an angle formed by two lines that intersect outside a circle is half the difference of the measures of the intercepted arcs." In Case 2 of the theorem, the two lines are a tangent line and a secant line. Use the diagram to prove Theorem 10-11, Case 2.

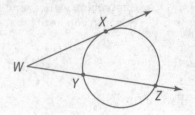

Given: Secants $\overrightarrow{WZ}$ and $\overrightarrow{WX}$

Prove: $m\angle W = \frac{1}{2}(m\widehat{XZ} - m\widehat{XY})$

EXAMPLE 3

Try It! Use Secants and Tangents to Solve Problems

3. **a.** What is $m\widehat{WX}$?

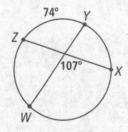

b. What is $m\angle PSQ$?

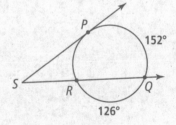

HABITS OF MIND

Look for Relationships What is the same and what is different about angles formed by intersecting chords, intersecting secants, intersecting tangents, and intersecting secants and tangents? © MP.7

EXAMPLE 4

Try It! **Develop Chord Length Relationships**

4. What is the value of *y*?

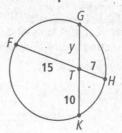

EXAMPLE 5

Try It! **Use Segment Relationships to Find Lengths**

5. **a.** What is the value of *a*?   **b.** What is *EC*?

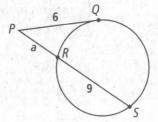
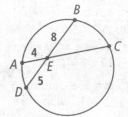

HABITS OF MIND

Generalize Theorem 10-12 states, "For a given point and circle, the product of the lengths of the two segments from the point to the circle is constant along any line through the point and circle."

Draw a circle with two segments that intersect outside the circle at point *P*. Then draw a circle with two chords that intersect inside the circle at point *Q*. What is the same about the lengths of the segments? What is different?
© MP.8

Do You UNDERSTAND?

1. **ESSENTIAL QUESTION** How are the measures of angles, arcs, and segments formed by intersecting secant lines related?

2. **Error Analysis** Massimo is asked to find the value of *x*. What is his error? © MP.3

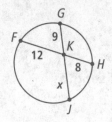

$GK \cdot FK = HK \cdot JK$
$12 \cdot 9 = 8 \cdot x$
$x = 13\frac{1}{2}$ ✗

3. **Vocabulary** How are *secants* and *tangents* to a circle alike and different?

4. **Construct Arguments** The rays shown are tangent to the circle. Show that $m\angle 1 = (x - 180)$. © MP.3

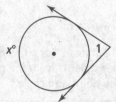

Do You KNOW HOW?

For Exercises 5 and 6, find each angle measure. Rays *QP* and *QR* are tangent to the circle in Exercise 6.

5. $m\angle BEC$

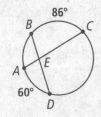

6. $m\angle PQR$

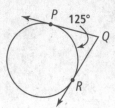

For Exercises 7 and 8, find each length. Ray *HJ* is tangent to the circle in Exercise 7.

7. *GF*

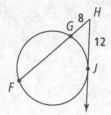

8. *LM*

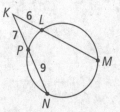

For Exercises 9 and 10, $\overline{AE}$ is tangent to ⊙*P*. Find each length.

9. *BC*

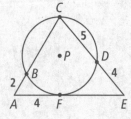

10. *EF*

EXPLORE & REASON

Consider a cube of cheese. If you slice straight down through the midpoints of four parallel edges of the cube, the outline of the newly exposed surface is a square.

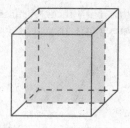

A. How would you slice the cube to expose a triangular surface?

B. Communicate Precisely How would you slice the cube to expose a triangular surface with the greatest possible area? Ⓒ **MP.6**

HABITS OF MIND

Use Structure How could you slice a cube to expose a rectangle that is not a square? Ⓒ **MP.7**

EXAMPLE 1

Try It! Develop Euler's Formula

1. How many faces, vertices, and edges do the pyramids have? Name at least three patterns you notice.

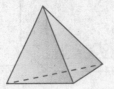   

EXAMPLE 2

Try It! Apply Euler's Formula

2. a. A polyhedron has 12 faces and 30 edges. How many vertices does it have?

   b. Can a polyhedron have 4 faces, 5 vertices, and 8 edges? Explain.

HABITS OF MIND

Reason Could a polyhedron ever have the same number of vertices and edges? Explain. © MP.2

EXAMPLE 3

Try It! Describe a Cross Section

3.

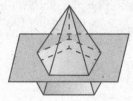

a. What shape is the cross section shown?

b. What shape is the cross section if the plane is perpendicular to the base and passes through the vertex of the pyramid?

EXAMPLE 4

Try It! Draw a Cross Section

4. **a.** Draw the cross section of a plane intersecting the tetrahedron through the top vertex and perpendicular to the base.

b. Draw the cross section of a plane intersecting a hexagonal prism perpendicular to the base.

EXAMPLE 5

Try It! Rotate a Polygon to Form a Three-Dimensional Figure

5. a. What three-dimensional figure is formed by rotating equilateral triangle $\triangle ABC$ about $\overline{BD}$?

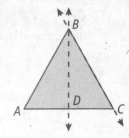

b. What three-dimensional figure is formed by rotating $\triangle ABC$ about $\overline{BC}$?

HABITS OF MIND

Communicate Precisely Can a polyhedron be formed by rotating a polygon about its side? Explain. Ⓒ **MP.6**

Do You UNDERSTAND?

1. **ESSENTIAL QUESTION** How are three-dimensional figures and polygons related?

2. **Error Analysis** Nicholas drew a figure to find a cross section of an icosahedron, a polyhedron with 20 faces. What is Nicholas's error? © MP.3

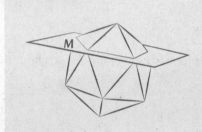

Because the plane that intersects the icosahedron is a rectangle, the cross section is a rectangle. ✗

3. **Reason** Can a polyhedron have 3 faces, 4 vertices, and 5 edges? Explain. © MP.2

Do You KNOW HOW?

For Exercises 4–7, complete the table.

	Faces	Vertices	Edges
4.	5	6	
5.	8		18
6.		12	44
7.	22	44	

8. What polygon is formed by the intersection of plane *N* and the octagonal prism shown?

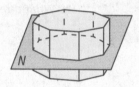

9. Describe the three-dimensional figure that is formed from rotating the isosceles right triangle about the hypotenuse.

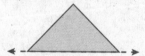

MODEL & DISCUSS

The Environmental Club has a piece of wire mesh that they want to form into an open-bottom and open-top compost bin.

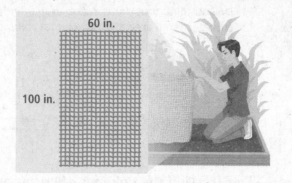

60 in.

100 in.

📖 SavvasRealize.com

A. Using one side as the height, describe how you can form a compost bin in the shape of a rectangular prism using all of the mesh with no overlap.

B. Construct Arguments Which height would result in the largest volume? Explain. ⓒ MP.3

C. Suppose you formed a cylinder using the same height as a rectangular prism. How would the volumes compare?

HABITS OF MIND

Reason How are the dimensions of the wire mesh related to the dimensions of the compost bin? ⓒ MP.2

EXAMPLE 1

Try It! Develop Cavalieri's Principle

1. Do you think that right and oblique cylinders that have the same height and cross-sectional area also have equal volume? Explain.

EXAMPLE 2

Try It! Find the Volumes of Prisms and Cylinders

2. **a.** A storage shed for firewood is in the shape of a triangular prism. The triangle has a base of 6 ft and a height of 4 feet. The shed is 2 ft from front to back. How would the volume of the storage shed change if the length of the triangular base is reduced by half?

b. Two food-storage canisters—one a right cylinder and one an oblique cylinder—both have diameters of 20 cm and heights of 25 cm. By Cavalieri's Principle, they have the same volume. How would the volume of the canisters change if the diameter is doubled?

HABITS OF MIND

Construct Arguments What is the same and what is different about finding area and finding volume? ⓒ MP.3

EXAMPLE 3

Try It! Apply Volume of a Prism to Solve Problems

3. Kathryn is using cans of juice to fill a cylindrical pitcher that is 11 in. tall and has a radius of 4 in. Each can of juice is 6 in. tall with a radius of 2 in. How many cans of juice will Kathryn need?

EXAMPLE 4

Try It! Solve Density Problems

4. Benito has 15 neon tetra fish in his aquarium. Each neon tetra requires at least 2 gallons of water. He is considering switching to an aquarium that is in the shape of a rectangular prism with a length of 24 in., a width of 12 in., and a height of 16 in. What is the maximum number of neon tetras that this aquarium can hold? (*Hint*: 1 gal = 231 in.^{3})

HABITS OF MIND

Communicate Precisely How can you confirm that your answers to Try Its 3 and 4 are reasonable? Ⓒ MP.6

EXAMPLE 5

Try It! Determine Whether Volume or Surface Area Best Describes Size

5. Describe a situation when surface area might be a better measure of size than volume.

HABITS OF MIND

Communicate Precisely To estimate the volume of wood in the trunk of a tall, straight tree such as a giant sequoia, you can model the trunk as a cylinder. What quantities must you estimate and what assumptions will you need to make for your model? Ⓒ MP.6

Do You UNDERSTAND?

1. **ESSENTIAL QUESTION** How does the volume of a prism or cylinder relate to a cross section parallel to its base?

2. **Error Analysis** Juliana says that Cavalieri's Principle proves that the two prisms shown have the same volume. Explain Juliana's error. Ⓒ MP.3

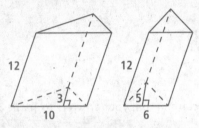

3. **Vocabulary** How are an oblique prism and an oblique cylinder alike and different?

4. **Reason** The circumference of the base of a cylinder is x, and the height of the cylinder is x. What expression gives the volume of the cylinder? Ⓒ MP.2

5. **Construct Arguments** Denzel kicks a large dent into a trash can and says that the volume does not change because of Cavalieri's Principle. Do you agree with Denzel? Explain. Ⓒ MP.3

Do You KNOW HOW?

For Exercises 6–11, find the volume of each figure. Round to the nearest tenth.

6.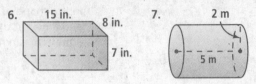

7.

8.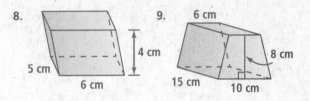

9.

10.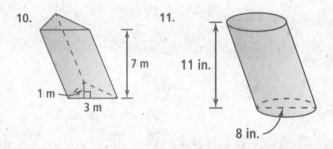

11.

12. Which figures have the same volume? Explain.

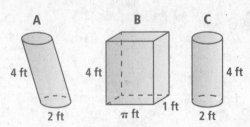

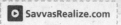

Box 'Em Up

With so many people and businesses shopping online, retailers, and especially e-retailers, ship more and more packages every day. Some of the products people order have unusual sizes and shapes and need custom packaging. Imagine how you might package a surfboard, or a snow blower, or even live crawfish to ship to someone's house!

Think about this during the Mathematical Modeling in 3 Acts lesson.

MATHEMATICAL MODELING IN 3 ACTS

ACT 1 **Identify the Problem**

1. What is the first question that comes to mind after watching the video?

2. Write down the main question you will answer about what you saw in the video.

3. Make an initial conjecture that answers this main question.

4. Explain how you arrived at your conjecture.

5. What information will be useful to know to answer the main question? How can you get it? How will you use that information?

ACT 2 Develop a Model

6. Use the math that you have learned in this Topic to refine your conjecture.

ACT 3 Interpret the Results

7. Did your refined conjecture match the actual answer exactly? If not, what might explain the difference?

EXPLORE & REASON

Consider the cube and pyramid.

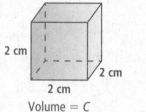

2 cm
2 cm
2 cm
Volume = C

1 cm
2 cm
2 cm
Volume = P

A. How many pyramids could you fit inside the cube? Explain.

B. Write an equation that shows the relationship between C and P.

C. **Look for Relationships** Make a conjecture about the volume of any pyramid. Explain your reasoning. Ⓒ MP.7

HABITS OF MIND

Use Structure Does the same pattern you found in Part A apply to other types of prisms and pyramids? Do you think the mathematical rule you found in Part B applies to all pyramids and prisms with the same size base? Ⓒ MP.7

EXAMPLE 1

Try It! Apply Cavalieri's Principle to Pyramids and Cones

1. Is it possible to use only Cavalieri's Principle to show that a cone and a cylinder have equal volumes? Explain.

EXAMPLE 2

Try It! Find the Volumes of Pyramids and Cones

2. a. What is the volume of a cone with base diameter 14 and height 16?

b. What is the volume of a pyramid with base area 10 and height 7?

HABITS OF MIND

Use Appropriate Tools What mathematical tools are helpful when solving problems about cones and pyramids? © MP.5

EXAMPLE 3

Try It! Apply the Volumes of Pyramids to Solve Problems

3. A rectangular pyramid has a base that is three times as long as it is wide. The volume of the pyramid is 75 ft³ and the height is 3 ft. What is the perimeter of the base?

EXAMPLE 4

Try It! Apply the Volumes of Cones to Solve Problems

4. A cone has a volume of 144π and a height of 12.

   a. What is the radius of the base?

   b. If the radius of the cone is tripled, what is the new volume? What is the relationship between the volumes of the two cones?

EXAMPLE 5

Try It! Measure a Composite Figure

5. A cone-shaped hole is drilled into a prism. The height of the triangular base of the prism is 12 cm. What is the volume of the remaining figure? Round to the nearest tenth.

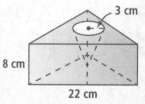

3 cm

8 cm

22 cm

HABITS OF MIND

Communicate Precisely How do you know that your solutions are reasonable? ⓒ MP.6

Do You UNDERSTAND?

1. **ESSENTIAL QUESTION** How are the formulas for volume of a pyramid and volume of a cone alike?

2. Error Analysis Zhang is finding the height of a square pyramid with a base side length of 9 and a volume of 162. What is his error? © **MP.3**

$$V = Bh$$
$$162 = 9^2(h)$$
$$h = 2$$ ✗

3. Reason A cone and cylinder have the same radius and volume. If the height of the cone is h, what is the height of the cylinder? © **MP.2**

4. Construct Arguments Do you have enough information to compute the volume of the cone? Explain. © **MP.3**

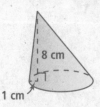
8 cm
1 cm

Do You KNOW HOW?

For Exercises 5–10, find the volume of each figure. Round to the nearest tenth. Assume that all angles in each polygonal base are congruent.

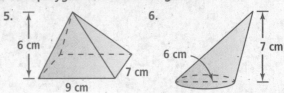

5.
6 cm
9 cm
7 cm

6.
6 cm
7 cm

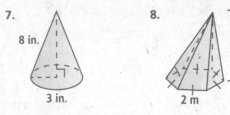

7.
8 in.
3 in.

8.
5 m
2 m

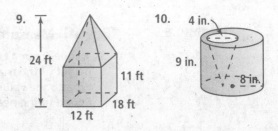

9.
24 ft
11 ft
18 ft
12 ft

10.
4 in.
9 in.
8 in.

11. A solid metal square pyramid with a base side length of 6 in. and height of 9 in. is melted down and recast as a square pyramid with a height of 4 in. What is the base side length of the new pyramid?

CRITIQUE & EXPLAIN

Ricardo estimates the volume of a sphere with radius 2 by placing the sphere inside a cylinder and placing two cones inside the sphere. He says that the volume of the sphere is less than 16π and greater than $\frac{16}{3}\pi$.

A. Do you agree with Ricardo? Explain.

B. Reason How might you estimate the volume of the sphere? © **MP.2**

HABITS OF MIND

Make Sense and Persevere What other figures could you contain within a sphere? © **MP.1**

EXAMPLE 1

Try It! Explore the Volume of a Sphere

1. Find the volumes of the three solids. What do you notice?

 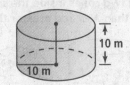 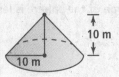

EXAMPLE 2

Try It! Use the Volumes of Spheres to Solve Problems

2. What is the largest volume a sphere can have if it is covered by 6 m² of fabric?

HABITS OF MIND

Use Structure Do cross sections parallel to the base of a half sphere, cylinder, or cone ever have zero area? Explain. © MP.7

EXAMPLE 3

Try It! Find the Volumes of Hemispheres

3. a. What is the volume of a hemisphere with radius 3 ft?

b. What is the volume of a hemisphere with diameter 13 cm?

EXAMPLE 4

Try It! Find the Volumes of Composite Figures

4. What is the volume of the space between the sphere and the cylinder?

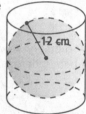

12 cm

HABITS OF MIND

Make Sense and Persevere How do you know if a plane divides a sphere into equal volumes? Explain. © MP.1

Do You UNDERSTAND?

1. **ESSENTIAL QUESTION** How does the volume of a sphere relate to the volumes of other solids?

2. **Error Analysis** Reagan is finding the volume of the sphere. What is her error? © **MP.3**

$$S.A. = \frac{4}{3}\pi r^3$$

$$S.A. = \frac{4}{3} \cdot \pi \cdot 3^3$$

$$S.A. \approx 113.1 \text{ square units}$$

3. **Vocabulary** How does a great circle define a hemisphere?

4. **Reason** The radius of a sphere, the base radius of a cylinder, and the base radius of a cone are r. What is the height of the cylinder if the volume of the cylinder is equal to the volume of the sphere? What is the height of the cone if the volume of the cone is equal to the volume of the sphere? © **MP.2**

Do You KNOW HOW?

For Exercises 5 and 6, find the surface area of each solid.

5.

6.

For Exercises 7 and 8, find the volume of each solid.

7.

8.

9. Find the volume of the largest sphere that can fit entirely in the rectangular prism.

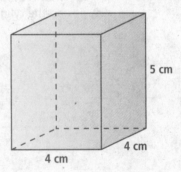

5 cm

4 cm

4 cm

10. Find the volume and surface area of a sphere with radius 1.

EXPLORE & REASON

Allie spins the spinner and draws one card without looking. She gets a 3 on the spinner and the 3 card. Then she sets the card aside, spins again, and draws another card.

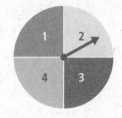 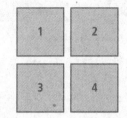

A. Is it possible for Allie to get a 3 on her second spin? On her second card? Explain.

B. **Construct Arguments** How does getting the 3 card on her first draw affect the probability of getting the 2 card on her second draw? Explain. © MP.3

HABITS OF MIND

Look for Relationships How are the results from the spinner related to the results from the cards? Explain. © MP.7

EXAMPLE 1

Try It! Find Probabilities of Mutually Exclusive Events

1. A box contains 100 balls. Thirty of the balls are purple and 10 are orange. If you select one of the balls at random, what is the probability of each of the following events?

   a. The ball is purple or orange.

   b. The ball is not purple and not orange.

EXAMPLE 2

Try It! Find the Probabilities of Non-Mutually Exclusive Events

2. A video game screen is a rectangle with dimensions 34 cm and 20 cm. A starship on the screen is made of two circles with radius 6 cm, and overlapping area of 20 cm². A black hole appears randomly on the screen. What is the probability that it appears within the starship?

HABITS OF MIND

Generalize Explain in your own words the meaning of mutually exclusive events. Include examples. © MP.8

EXAMPLE 3

Try It! Identify Independent Events

3. There are 10 cards in a box, 5 black and 5 red. Two cards are selected from the box, one at a time.

   a. A card is chosen at random and then replaced. Another card is chosen. Does the color of the first card chosen affect the possibilities of the second card chosen? Explain.

   b. A card is chosen at random and not replaced. Another card is chosen. Does the color of the first card chosen affect the possibilities of the second card chosen? Explain

EXAMPLE 4

Try It! Find Probabilities of Independent Events

4. You spin the spinner two times. Assume that the probability of Blue (B) each spin is $\frac{1}{3}$ and the probability of Orange (O) each spin is $\frac{2}{3}$. What is the probability of getting the same color both times? Explain.

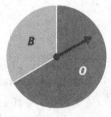

HABITS OF MIND

Make Sense and Persevere Explain the difference between mutually exclusive events and independent events. © **MP.1**

Do You UNDERSTAND?

1. **ESSENTIAL QUESTION** How does describing events as independent or mutually exclusive affect how you find probabilities?

2. **Reason** Two marbles are chosen, one at a time, from a bag containing 6 marbles, 4 red marbles and 2 green marbles. Suppose the first marble chosen is green. Is the probability that the second marble will be red greater if the first marble is returned to the bag or if it is not returned to the bag? Explain. © **MP.2**

3. **Error Analysis** The probability that Deshawn plays basketball (event B) after school is 20%. The probability that he talks to friends (event T) after school is 45%. He says that $P(B$ or $T)$ is 65%. Explain Deshawn's error. © **MP.3**

4. **Vocabulary** What is the difference between mutually exclusive events and independent events?

Do You KNOW HOW?

5. A bag contains 40 marbles. Eight are green and 2 are blue. You select one marble at random. What is the probability of each event?

   a. The marble is green or blue.

   b. The marble is not green and not blue.

6. A robot at a carnival booth randomly tosses a dart at a square target with 8 inch sides and a circle with a 3 inch radius in the middle. To the nearest whole percent, what is the probability that the dart will land in the circle?

For Exercises 7 and 8, assume that you roll a standard number cube two times.

7. What is the probability of rolling an even number on the first roll and a number less than 3 on the second roll?

8. What is the probability of rolling an odd number on the first roll and a number greater than 3 on the second roll?

EXPLORE & REASON

At Central High School, 85% of all senior girls attended and 65% of all senior boys attended the Spring Dance. Of all attendees, 20% won a prize.

A. Assuming that the number of senior girls at Central High School is about equal to the number of senior boys, estimate the probability that a randomly selected senior won a prize at the dance. Explain.

B. Construct Arguments If you knew whether the selected student was a boy or a girl, would your estimate change? Explain. © MP.3

HABITS OF MIND

Look for Relationships How would the probability that a senior selected at random won a prize be different if only 60% of senior girls and 50% of senior boys attended the dance? Explain. © MP.7

EXAMPLE 1

Try It! Understand Conditional Probability

1. A student committee is being formed to decide how after-school activities will be funded. The committee members are selected at random from current club members. The frequency table shows the current club membership data.

Monday Club Membership by Grade				
	Drama	Science	Art	Total
Sophomore	3	9	24	36
Junior	6	18	16	40
Senior	8	13	18	39
Total	17	40	58	115

a. What is the probability that a member of the drama club is a sophomore, $P(\text{sophomore} \mid \text{drama})$?

b. What is the probability that a sophomore is a member of the drama club, $P(\text{drama} \mid \text{sophomore})$? Is $P(\text{sophomore} \mid \text{drama})$ the same as $P(\text{drama} \mid \text{sophomore})$? Explain

EXAMPLE 2

Try It! Use the Test for Independence

2. The table below shows the vehicles in a parking garage one afternoon. A vehicle in the garage will be selected at random. Let R represent "the vehicle is red" and C represent "the vehicle is a car." Are the events R and C independent or dependent? Explain.

	Car	Van	Pickup	Totals
Red	5	0	2	7
White	0	0	2	2
Black	6	3	4	13
Totals	11	3	8	22

- -

HABITS OF MIND

Make Sense and Persevere Suppose you know that events A and B are independent, and you find that $P(B \mid A) = P(A \mid B)$. What else do you know? ⓒ **MP.1**

EXAMPLE 3

Try It! Apply the Conditional Probability Formula

3. What is the probability that a surveyed student plans to attend but is not a fan of the group?

Concert Survey Results

Students who plan to attend concert

- 70% of students plan to attend,
- 80% of students who plan to attend are fans of the band.

Students who do not plan to attend

- 30% of students do not plan to attend,
- 25% are fans of the band.

EXAMPLE 4

Try It! Use Conditional Probability to Make a Decision

4. The marketer also has data from desktop computers. Which product is most likely to be purchased after a related search?

Computer Search and Buying Behavior
(% of computer-based site visitors)

Product	Search	Search & Buy
J	35%	10%
K	28%	9%
L	26%	8%
M	24%	5%

HABITS OF MIND

Communicate Precisely Compare the formula used in Example 3, $P(A \text{ and } B) = P(A) \cdot P(B \mid A)$, to the formula used in Example 4, $P(B \mid A) = \frac{P(A \text{ and } B)}{P(A)}$. How are they related? When would you use each formula? Ⓒ MP.6

Do You UNDERSTAND?

1. **ESSENTIAL QUESTION** How are conditional probability and independence related in experiments?

2. **Vocabulary** How is the sample space for $P(B \mid A)$ different from the sample space for $P(B)$?

3. **Vocabulary** Why does the definition of $P(B \mid A)$ have the condition that $P(A) \neq 0$?

4. **Use Structure** Why is $P(A) \cdot P(B \mid A) = P(B) \cdot P(A \mid B)$? © MP.7

5. **Error Analysis** Jamal knows that $P(R) = 0.8$, $P(B) = 0.2$, and $P(R \text{ and } B) = 0.05$. Explain Taylor's error. © MP.3

$$P(B \mid R) = \frac{0.05}{0.2}$$
$$= 0.25$$

6. **Reason** At a sports camp, a coach wants to find the probability that a soccer player is a local camper. Because 40% of the students in the camp are local, the coach reasons that the probability is 0.4. Is his conclusion justified? Explain. © MP.2

Do You KNOW HOW?

7. Let $P(A) = \frac{3}{4}$, $P(B) = \frac{2}{3}$, and $P(A \text{ and } B) = \frac{1}{2}$. Find each probability.

   a. What is $P(B \mid A)$?

   b. What is $P(A \mid B)$?

8. Students randomly generate two digits from 0 to 9 to create a number between 0 and 99. Are the events "first digit 5" and "second digit 6" independent or dependent in each case? What is $P(56)$ in each experiment?

   a. The digits may not be repeated.

   b. The digits may be repeated.

9. Suppose that you select one card at random from the set of 6 cards below.

Let B represent the event "select a blue card" and T represent the event "select a card with a 3." Are B and T independent events? Explain your reasoning.

Place Your Guess

A coin toss is a popular way to decide between two options or settle a dispute. The coin toss is popular because it is a simple and unbiased way of deciding. Assuming the coin being tossed is a fair coin, both parties have an equally likely chance of winning.

What other methods could you use to decide between two choices fairly? Think about this during the Mathematical Modeling in 3 Acts lesson.

ACT 1 ▶ **Identify the Problem**

1. What is the first question that comes to mind after watching the video?

2. Write down the main question you will answer about what you saw in the video.

3. Make an initial conjecture that answers this main question.

4. Explain how you arrived at your conjecture.

5. What information will be useful to know to answer the main question? How can you get it? How will you use that information?

ACT 2 Develop a Model

6. Use the math that you have learned in this Topic to refine your conjecture.

ACT 3 Interpret the Results

7. Did your refined conjecture match the actual answer exactly? If not, what might explain the difference?

EXPLORE & REASON

Holly, Tia, Kenji, and Nate are eligible to be officers of the Honor Society. Two of the four students will be chosen at random as president and vice-president. The table summarizes the possible outcomes.

Honor Society Officers

		Vice-President		
		Holly	Tia	Kenji	Nate
President	Holly	–	HT	HK	HN
	Tia	TH	–	TK	TN
	Kenji	KH	KT	–	KN
	Nate	NH	NT	NK	–

A. Holly wants to be an officer with her best friend Tia. How many outcomes make up this event?

B. How many outcomes show Holly as president and Tia as vice-president?

C. **Generalize** How many outcomes have only one of them as an officer? Explain. © MP.8

HABITS OF MIND

Make Sense and Persevere How could you use the table to calculate the probability that both Holly and Tia will be officers? © MP.1

EXAMPLE 1

Try It! Use the Fundamental Counting Principle

1. The car that Ms. Garcia is buying comes with a choice of 3 trim lines (standard, sport, or luxury), 2 types of transmission (automatic or manual), and 8 colors. How many different option packages does Ms. Garcia have to choose from? Explain.

EXAMPLE 2

Try It! Find the Number of Permutations

2. How many possibilities are there for each playlist?

   a. Gabriela's 4 favorite songs

   b. 5 of the 10 most popular songs

HABITS OF MIND

Communicate Precisely Explain how the Fundamental Counting principle can be used to find the number of ways to arrange 5 different colored beads on a string. Ⓒ MP.6

EXAMPLE 3

Try It! Find the Number of Combinations

3. How many ways can a camper choose 5 activities from the 10 available activities at the summer camp?

EXAMPLE 4

Try It! Use Permutations and Combinations to Find Probabilities

4. Using the data from Example 4 shown below, what is the probability that the 5 students' names end with a vowel?

HABITS OF MIND

Look for Relationships What is the relationship between $_{10}P_5$ and $_{10}C_5$? Is the number of permutations always greater than the number of combinations? © MP.7

Do You UNDERSTAND?

1. **ESSENTIAL QUESTION** How are permutations and combinations useful when finding probabilities?

2. **Use Structure** How is the formula for combinations related to the formula for a permutations? Ⓒ **MP.7**

3. **Vocabulary** Why is it important to distinguish between a *permutation* and a *combination* when counting possible outcomes?

4. **Look for Relationships** How is $_9C_2$ related to $_9C_7$? Explain. How can you generalize this observation for any values of n and r? Ⓒ **MP.7**

5. **Error Analysis** Explain Beth's error. Ⓒ **MP.3**

$$\frac{_3P_3}{_5P_3} = \frac{3!}{\frac{5!}{(5-3)!}} = \frac{3!}{5!2!} = \frac{1}{40}$$ ✗

6. **Construct Arguments** A company wants to form a committee of 4 people from its 12 employees. How can you use combinations to find the probability that the 4 people newest to the company will be selected? Ⓒ **MP.3**

Do You KNOW HOW?

Do the possible outcomes represent permutations or combinations?

7. Jennifer will invite 3 of her 10 friends to a concert.

8. Tamisha must decide how she and her 3 friends will sit at the concert.

Find the number of permutations.

9. How many ways can 12 runners in a race finish first, second, and third?

Find the number of combinations.

10. In how many ways can 11 contestants for an award be narrowed down to 3 finalists?

11. How many different ways can a 4-person team can be chosen from a group of 8 people?

Students will be chosen at random for school spirit awards. There are 6 athletes and 8 non-athletes who are eligible for 2 possible prizes. What is each probability?

12. P(both prizes are awarded to athletes)

13. P(both prizes are awarded to non-athletes)

14. P(no prize is awarded to an athlete)

15. P(no prize is awarded to a non-athlete)

16. Explain how Exercises 12 and 13 are similar to Exercises 14 and 15.

EXPLORE & REASON

Mr. and Mrs. Mason have three children. Assume that the probability of having a baby girl is 0.5 and the probability of having a baby boy is also 0.5.

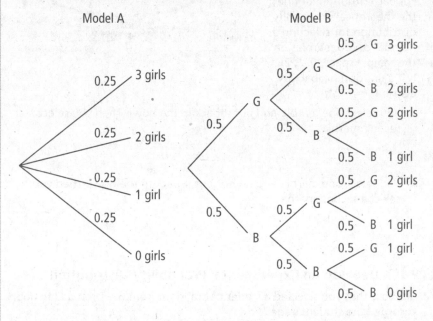

Model A

Model B

A. Reason Which model represents the situation correctly, Model A or Model B? Explain. © MP.2

B. What is the probability that Mr. and Mrs. Mason have 3 girls?

C. Compare the probability that the Masons' first child was a boy and they then had two girls to the probability that their first two children were girls and they then had a boy. Does the order affect the probabilities? Explain.

HABITS OF MIND

Look for Relationships Which combinations of children are most common? Is one order of this combination more likely? Explain. © MP.7

EXAMPLE 1

Try It! Develop a Theoretical Probability Distribution

1. You select two marbles at random from the bowl. For each situation, define the theoretical probability distribution for selecting a number of red marbles on the sample space {0, 1, 2}. Is it a uniform probability distribution?

a. You select one marble and put it back in the bowl. Then you select a second marble.

b. You select one marble and do not put it back in the bowl. Then you select a second marble.

EXAMPLE 2

Try It! Develop an Experimental Probability Distribution

2. Suppose that you selected a student at random from the Drama Club and recorded the student's age.

Ages of Students in Drama Club				
Age	14	15	16	17	18
Students	4	7	10	7	9

a. Define an experimental probability distribution on the sample space {14, 15, 16, 17, 18}.

b. Graph the probability distribution you defined.

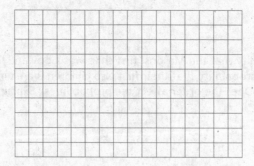

- -
HABITS OF MIND

Look for Relationships Compare the graph of a uniform probability distribution with the graph of a non-uniform distribution. ⓒ MP.7

EXAMPLE 3

Try It! Binomial Experiments

3. Is the experiment a binomial experiment? If so, find the probability of success. Explain.

   a. You select one card at random from a set of 7 cards, 4 labeled A and 3 labeled B. Then you select another card at random from the cards that remain. For each selection, success is that the card is labeled A.

   b. You roll a standard number cube 4 times. Assume that each time you roll the number cube, each number is equally likely to come up. For each roll, success is getting an even number.

EXAMPLE 4

Try It! Probabilities in a Binomial Experiment

4. A grocery store gives away scratch-off cards with a purchase of more than $100. Terrell has 5 scratch-off cards. To the nearest tenth of a percent, what is the probability that Terrell has more than 3 winning cards? Explain.

HABITS OF MIND

Use Structure Explain why $_nC_r$ appears in the formula for the probability of a binomial experiment. © MP.7

Do You UNDERSTAND?

1. **ESSENTIAL QUESTION** What does a probability distribution tell you about an experiment?

2. **Vocabulary** What are the characteristics of a *binomial experiment*?

3. **Error Analysis** A regular tetrahedron has four triangular sides, with one of the letters A, B, C, and D on each side. Assume that if you roll the tetrahedron, each of the letters is equally likely to end up on the bottom. {A, B, C, D} is a sample space for the experiment. Rochelle was asked to find the theoretical probability distribution for the experiment. Explain and correct the error. ⓒ MP.3

$P(A) = 0.3$
$P(B) = 0.3$
$P(C) = 0.3$
$P(D) = 0.3$ ✗

Do You KNOW HOW?

Graph the probability distribution P.

4. Theoretical probabilities from selecting a student at random from a group of 3 students, Jack, Alani, and Malik

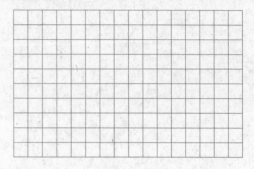

5. Probabilities from flipping a fair coin 3 times and counting the number of heads. The sample space is the set of numbers 0, 1, 2, 3. $P(0) = 0.125$, $P(1) = 0.375$, $P(2) = 0.375$, $P(3) = 0.125$

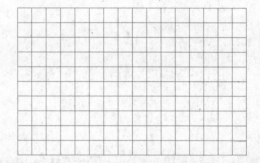

A bag contains 5 balls: 3 green, 1 red, and 1 yellow. You select a ball at random 4 times, replacing the ball after each selection. Calculate the theoretical probability of each event to the nearest whole percent.

6. getting a green ball exactly 3 times

7. getting a green ball exactly 4 times

8. getting a green ball at least 3 times

9. getting a yellow ball twice

10. getting only red and green balls

EXPLORE & REASON

A company has 20 employees whose hourly wages are shown in the bar graph.

A. An employee is chosen at random. What is the probability that his or her hourly wage is $12? $25? $50?

B. What is the mean hourly wage? Explain your method.

C. Construct Arguments Is the mean a good description of the typical hourly wage at this company? Explain. ⓒ **MP.3**

HABITS OF MIND

Reasoning Compare the mean hourly wage to the median hourly wage. Which would be a more useful value to know if you want to estimate the total amount the company pays its employees? Explain. ⓒ **MP.2**

EXAMPLE 1

Try It! Evaluate and Apply Expected Value

1. The table shows data on sales in one month for each item on a restaurant menu.

Meal	Profit per Serving	Percent Sold
Stew	$0.34	12%
Soup	$0.41	7%
Lasagna	$0.64	45%
Chili	$0.73	36%

   a. What would happen to the expected value if fewer people ordered chili and more people ordered stew? Explain.

   b. Suppose the restaurant's profit on an order of stew increased by $0.05 and the profit on an order of chili decreased by $0.05. How would these changes affect the expected profit per meal?

EXAMPLE 2

Try It! Find Expected Payoffs

2. A charity is considering a fundraising event in which donors will pay $1 to spin the wheel 3 times. What is the expected payoff for the person making the donation?

EVEN THREES
Spin 3 times.
Get 3 even numbers.
Win an item worth $4.

HABITS OF MIND

Construct Arguments What happens to expected value when the value of an outcome increases while its probability decreases? © MP.3

EXAMPLE 3

Try It! Use Expected Values to Evaluate Strategies

3. The insurance company in Example 3 also offers optional safety glass coverage. Annual windshield repair statistics are: 50% no repairs ($0), 30% minor repairs ($50), and 20% full replacement ($300). Which plan for optional safety glass coverage has the lower expected cost?

Plan	Premium ($)	Deductible ($)
C	50	200
D	100	0

EXAMPLE 4

Try It! Use Binomial Probability to Find Expected Value

4. A carnival game has 4 orange lights and 1 green light that flash rapidly one at a time in a random order. When a player pushes a button, the game stops, leaving one light on. If the light is green, the player wins a prize. Copy and complete the table, then determine the number of prizes that a player can expect to win if the game is played 4 times.

Number of Green Lights (wins)	Probability
0	$_4C_0(0.2)^0(0.8)^4 = $ ▦
1	$_4C\ (0.2)\ (0.8)\ = $ ▦
2	$C\ (0.2)\ (0.8)\ = $ ▦
3	$C\ (0.2)\ (0.8)\ = $ ▦
4	$C\ (0.2)\ (0.8)\ = $ ▦

HABITS OF MIND

Generalize When do you add expected values and when do you compare individual expected values? Explain. ⓒ MP.8

Do You UNDERSTAND?

1. **ESSENTIAL QUESTION** What does expected value tell about situations involving probability?

2. **Error Analysis** Benjamin is finding the expected value of the number of heads when tossing a fair coin 10 times. What is Benjamin's error? © **MP.3**

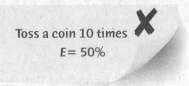

Toss a coin 10 times **X**

$E = 50\%$

3. **Construct Arguments** A carnival game costs $1 to play. The expected payout for each play of this game is $1.12. Should the carnival operators modify the game in way? Explain. © **MP.3**

4. **Reason** The students in Ms. Kwan's class are raising money to help earthquake victims. They expect to raise $0.52 for each raffle ticket they sell. If each raffle ticket is sold for $2, what can you conclude? © **MP.2**

5. **Reason** A spinner is divided into 6 equal-sized sectors, numbered 1, 1, 1, 4, 7, and 10. Is the expected value of a spin the same as the mean of the numbers? Explain. © **MP.2**

Do You KNOW HOW?

6. What is the expected value when rolling a standard number cube?

7. What is the expected value when rolling two standard number cubes?

8. A travel website reports that in a particular South American city, the probability of rain on any day in April is 40%. What is the expected number of rainy days in this city during the month of April?

9. You buy an airplane ticket for $900. You discover that if you cancel or rebook your vacation flight to Europe, you will be charged an extra $300. There is a 20% chance that you will have to rebook your flight.

   a. What is the expected value of the cost of the ticket?

   b. Is the expected value the amount you will pay to book the ticket whether or not you have to rebook? Explain.

10. A child-care service charges families an hourly rate based upon the age of the child. Their hourly rate per child is $20 per hour for infants less than 1 year old, $18 for toddlers 1 to 3 years old, $15 per hour children 3 or more years old. The ratio of infants : toddlers : 3+ years is 2 : 3 : 5. What is the expected charge per child per hour?

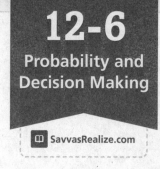
CRITIQUE & EXPLAIN

Your friend offers to play the following game with you. "If the product of the rolls of two number cubes is 10 or less, I win. If not, you win!"

A. If you were to play the game many times, what percent of games would you expect to win?

B. Is the game fair? Should you take the offer? Explain.

C. Make Sense and Persevere Suggest a way to change the game from fair to unfair, or vice versa, while still using the product of the two number cubes. Explain. © MP.1

HABITS OF MIND

Use Structure Change the game from using products to using a different mathematical number operation. Can you make the game fair? Explain your reasoning. © MP.7

EXAMPLE 1

Try It! Use Probability to Make Fair Decisions

1. Your trainer creates training programs for you. How can you use index cards to randomly choose the following: Strength training 1 day per week; Cardio training 2 days per week, with no consecutive days; Swimming 1 day per week.

EXAMPLE 2

Try It! Determine Whether a Decision Is Fair or Unfair

2. Justice and Tamika use the same 3 cards, but change the game. In each round, a player draws a card and replaces it, and then the other player draws. The differences between the two cards are used to score each round. Order matters, so the difference can be negative. Is each game fair? Explain.

   a. If the difference between the first and second cards is 2, Justice gets a point. Otherwise Tamika gets a point.

   b. They take turns drawing first. Each round, the first player to draw subtracts the second player's number from her own and the result is added to her total score.

EXAMPLE 3

Try It! Make a Decision Based on Expected Value

3.

Model TAB5000	Model TAB5001
• Cost to produce: $100 • Price: $150 • 5% fail within first year • Replacement cost to company: $130	• Cost to produce: $105 • Price: $150 • 1% fail within first year (estimate) • Replacement cost to company: $135

Additional data is collected for the TAB5000 and TAB5001. The manufacturing cost and the replacement cost for the TAB5001 remain unchanged.

a. The production and replacement costs for the TAB5000 increased by $1-. What would the expected profit be for the TAB5000?

b. The failure rate for the TAB5001 increased by 1%. What would the expected profit be for the TAB5001?

c. As a consultant for the company, what would you recommend they do to maximize their profit?

HABITS OF MIND

Construct Arguments When do you need to compute and compare expected values instead of just comparing probabilities? Explain. © MP.3

EXAMPLE 4

Try It! Use a Binomial Distribution to Make Decisions

4. A play calls for a crowd of 12 extras with non-speaking parts. Because 10% of the extras have not shown up in the past, the director selects 15 students as extras. Find the probabilities that 12 extras show up to the performance, 15 extras show up to the performance, and more than 12 extras show up to the performance.

EXAMPLE 5

Try It! Understanding False Positive and False Negative Results

5. A Chemistry teacher gives a pop quiz to see if the students read last night's assignment. The teacher expects a student to pass the quiz if the reading has been completed.

Chemistry Quiz Results			
	Passed	Failed	Totals
Completed Reading	95	1	96
Incomplete Reading	7	7	14
Totals	102	8	110

a. What represents false positives and false negatives for the data?

b. What risk does a false value present?

HABITS OF MIND

Use Structure What three expressions are multiplied together in the binomial probability formula and what do they represent? Ⓒ MP.7

Do You UNDERSTAND?

1. **ESSENTIAL QUESTION** How can you use probability to make decisions?

2. **Reason** How can you use random numbers to simulate rolling a standard number cube? ©**MP.2**

3. **Error Analysis** Explain the error in Diego's reasoning. ©**MP.3**

If a game uses random numbers, it is always fair.

4. **Use Structure** Describe what conditions are needed for a fair game. ©**MP.7**

5. **Use Appropriate Tools** Explain how you can visualize probability distributions to help you make decisions. ©**MP.5**

6. **Reason** Why must the expected value of a fair game of chance equal zero? ©**MP.2**

Do You KNOW HOW?

7. A teacher assigns each of 30 students a a unique number from 1 to 30. The teacher uses the random numbers shown to select students for presentations. Which student was selected first? second?

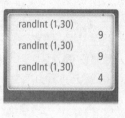

randInt (1,30)	9
randInt (1,30)	9
randInt (1,30)	4

8. Three friends are at a restaurant and they all want the last slice of pizza. Identify three methods involving probability that they can use to determine who gets the last slice. Explain mathematically why each method will guarantee a fair decision.

9. Edgar rolls one number cube and Micah rolls two. If Edgar rolls a 6, he wins a prize. If Micah rolls a sum of 7, she gets a prize. Is this game fair? Explain.

10. The 10 parking spaces in the first row of the parking lot are reserved for the 12 members of the Student Council. Usually an average of ten percent of the Student Council does not drive to school dances. What is the probability that more members of the Student Council will drive to a dance than there are reserved parking spaces?